IN HONORED GLORY

ARLINGTON NATIONAL CEMETERY
THE FINAL POST

FOURTH EDITION

Philip Bigler

VANDAMERE
PRESS

Published by
Vandamere Press
P.O. Box 149
St. Petersburg, FL 33731
USA

Fourth Edition
Copyright 2005 by Vandamere Press

First Edition Printing History
First Printing December 1986
Second Printing August 1987
Third Printing April 1990
Fourth Printing April 1992
Second Edition Printing History
First Printing May 1994
Second Printing May 1996
Third Printing July 1997
Fourth Printing September 1998
Third Edition Printing History
First Printing May 1999
Second Printing June 2000
Third Printing January 2001
Fourth Printing September 2001
Fifth Printing January 2003
Sixth Printing May 2004
Fourth Edition Printing History
First Printing May 2005

ISBN 0-918339-67-7, hardcover
ISBN 0-918339-68-5, Paper

Cover photograph by Jerry Dreo

Dedicated in loving memory
to my parents

Cdr. Charles E. Bigler (USN)

&

Bernice R. Bigler

Their daily lives reflected the
dedication, sacrifice, and patriotism
of our nation's military families.

Section 7A, 113

In Memoriam

Major Otho Leroy Mimms
United States Air Force
& Eva Belle Mimms
Section 7, 9198-A

Col. Paul J. Walsh
United States Army
Section 60, 1435

MSgt. Fred Fisher
United States Marine Corps
Section 13, 14456

Evelyn Inez Dunson
Section 7, 10185-B

Philip J. Walsh
National Park Service
Arlington House

Acknowledgements

It has been over twenty years since the first edition of In Honored Glory was first published. During that time, Arlington National Cemetery has continued to expand as the demand for grave space has increased with the gradual passing of the World War II generation into history. On a personal note, I have buried both my parents and in-laws at Arlington. It is through their memory that I am constantly reminded of the sacrifice of those veterans and their spouses who willingly put aside careers, delayed families, and left home to prevent the triumph of tyranny. As historian Stephen Ambrose so astutely observed in The Victors: "…the American citizen soldiers knew the difference between right and wrong, and didn't want to live in a world in which wrong prevailed. So they fought, and won, and all of us, living and yet to be born, must be profoundly grateful."

So it is to Arlington National Cemetery where we come to give thanks to all of those who have sacrificed for our nation's ideals as well as to honor those brave servicemen and women who maintain this legacy of honor. It is my fondest hope that this book will pay tribute to all of those who serve in our nation's armed services and provide some solace and comfort to those who come to Arlington in grief to mourn the loss of America's sons and daughters. I would like to take this opportunity to express my thanks to the many individuals who provided assistance during the preparation of this book. First, I will be forever indebted to Raymond J. Costanzo, the former Superintendent of Arlington National Cemetery, who graciously gave his time, support, and encouragement to this project. I would also like to thank Tom Sherlock, Arlington's historian and my colleague for two years, for his help and guidance. Likewise, Thurmon Higginbotham and Gene Wilson were kind enough to share with me many of their personal experiences at Arlington during their long and accomplished careers.

I am particularly grateful to Lionel Harrell, a good friend and colleague, who continues to typify the professionalism, dignity, and compassion of all of those who work at Arlington National Cemetery.

The sentinels at the Tomb of the Unknown Soldier deserve special acknowledgment and recognition. My thanks go to S/SGT Ken Gordon and SP4 Brett Gookin. At the caisson platoon, 1SGT Michael Wilson was an outstanding resource in relating the history and duties of the regiment. At the Pentagon, Helene C. Stikkel was particularly helpful in providing photographs of the aftermath of September 11th.

My editor, Pat Berger, and my publisher, Art Brown, have worked diligently with me. Their suggestions and comments have been greatly welcomed and appreciated. Special thanks also to Jerry Dreo for his work on the cover photo and to Dick Cramer for his timely photographic assistance.

Judy Hynson at Stratford Hall Plantation graciously provided me with a series of remarkable letters from Robert and Mary Lee concerning Arlington while Phil Walsh at the National Park Service has helped me locate key government records. Wende Walsh has likewise provided important grammatical advice and literary suggestions. My wife, Linda, has been an exceptional proofreader, a loving friend, and an understanding spouse.

Finally, I am particularly grateful to Rebecca Stevens Davis, my assistant at the Madison Center at James Madison University. She has worked tirelessly on this manuscript and has selflessly devoted her time and energy to completing this project, and to Katie Overstreet for her excellent work on digitizing the books photographs and for her efforts in compiling the index. To all, my lasting appreciation and thanks.

TABLE OF CONTENTS

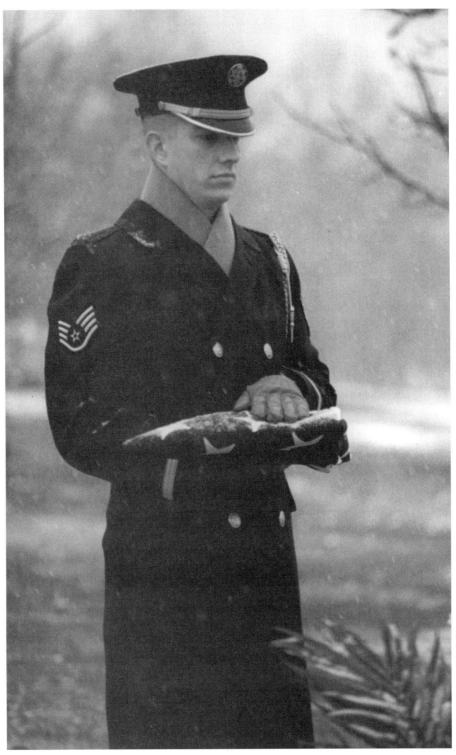

CHAPTER ONE

The Nation's Burial Ground

Each morning, the serenity of Arlington National Cemetery is temporarily interrupted by the sharp report of rifle volleys followed by the haunting notes of "Taps." An Armed Forces casket team adroitly folds an outstretched American flag into a triangle, which is then solemnly presented to a next of kin on behalf of the President of the United States. This same precise ceremony is repeated throughout the day, the nation's final tribute to its deceased veterans.

Arlington National Cemetery was carved out of the 1,100-acre plantation originally owned by George Washington Parke Custis and is now the most widely known of the 120 national cemeteries. Over 290,000 Americans are buried within the grounds - - the famous and the anonymous, generals and privates, presidents and politicians.

Overlooking the cemetery's 624 acres is the majestic, classical-revival Arlington House mansion, the antebellum home of the Confederate general, Robert E. Lee. Built in the early 19th century, the manor house was seized at the outset of the American Civil War. It was initially converted into a military headquarters for the Union Army but in 1864, in an act of vengeance, burials were begun around the mansion to prevent Lee from ever returning to his beloved home.

Nearby are endless rows of identical white headstones, marking the graves of over 16,000 federal soldiers who lost their lives during the Civil War. Appropriately known as the "Field of the Dead," the section bears a silent testimony to the incredible human toll of the nation's most divisive war. A short distance away, a stark, gray granite memorial erected over the commingled remains of 2,111 unknowns is further witness to that horrible loss.

Directly below the Arlington House mansion is the grave of President John F. Kennedy, one of the two American chief executives buried at the cemetery. The focal point of the memorial gravesite is the eternal flame that provides a powerful reminder of the continued legacy of the martyred President's ideals. Inscribed around the grave's ellipse are inspiring quotations from President Kennedy's 1961 inaugural address. His assassinated brother,

Robert F. Kennedy, is buried in an adjacent site.

In the distance is the Memorial Amphitheater, once called "America's Temple of Patriotism." The structure was originally built to accommodate the large Memorial Day crowds that annually gathered at the cemetery. Today, the Amphitheater is more commonly associated with the Tomb of the Unknown Soldier, undoubtedly the nation's most sacred shrine to American servicemen. In 1921, the World War I Unknown was buried on the plaza of the Amphitheater. Subsequently, anonymous soldiers from World War II and the Korean Conflict have similarly been interred, all perpetually guarded by a stoic sentinel from the 3rd United States Infantry, "the Old Guard." There is no unknown from the Vietnam War and the intended crypt for that soldier will forever remain empty. Some 2,000 ceremonies are conducted at the Tomb each year in honor of American soldiers.

Numerous monuments to American servicemen are located throughout Arlington Cemetery. The Mast of the U.S.S. Maine was erected near the graves of the sailors who were killed in the catastrophic explosion of the vessel in 1898; the Spanish-American Memorial pays tribute to those who lost their lives in the ensuing war with Spain. The Confederate Memorial commemorates the valor of Southern soldiers during the Civil War while the Argonne Cross represents members of the American Expeditionary Forces that liberated Europe during World War I.

Arlington has become the final resting place for many notables from

Chris Cross Photography

A World War II veteran is escorted to his final rest at Arlington National Cemetery

American history. Among these are General Philip Sheridan, the Union cavalry commander; General of the Armies John J. "Black Jack" Pershing, the highest ranking American military office; Joe Louis, the famed heavyweight champion; Earl Warren, the Chief Justice of the Supreme Court; and William Howard Taft, President of the United States. Dead from all of the nation's wars from the Revolution through the liberation of Iraq have also been buried at Arlington: soldiers who saw action during the climactic battle of Gettysburg or who landed on the beaches of Normandy or withstood the brutal siege at Khe Sanh. Others died exploring new realms, including Gus Grissom and Roger Chaffee aboard Apollo, Francis Scobee and Michael Smith on the Space Shuttle Challenger, and most recently astronauts Michael Anderson, Dave Brown and Laurel Clark from the Columbia mission. Tragic accidents and catastrophic disasters have similarly conspired to take the lives of other American servicemen: 21 Marines in a terrorist bombing in Lebanon, 18 sailors in a fire on the U.S.S. Forrestal, three crewmen in a crash during an aborted rescue effort of American hostages in Iran, and 64 victims from the September 11 terrorist attack on the Pentagon.

Each year, four million visitors make the pilgrimage to Arlington Cemetery, the nation's most hallowed burial ground. The thousands of Americans who are interred at the cemetery have their names inscribed in stone, but their deeds are recorded in the nation's history. Each headstone represents a story waiting to be told, a past to be remembered.

CHAPTER TWO

... A Most Lovely Spot, Overlooking the Potomac

—Henry Fleete

Martha Dandridge was only 16 at the time of her marriage to Daniel Parke Custis, a man 20 years her senior. It was not uncommon in colonial Virginia for women to marry so young. As planter William Byrd noted in his diary, "An old maid...[is] as scarce among us and reckoned as ominous as a blazing star." For the next seven years, Daniel and Martha made their home on the Custis plantation located on the Pamunkey River near the colonial capital of Williamsburg. Their marriage produced two offspring, John Parke and Martha.

Daniel Custis died suddenly in 1757, leaving Martha a young but wealthy widow with two fatherless children. Since death was an unfortunate but ever-present reality in the American colonies, mourning periods were necessarily brief, lasting only a few weeks. Thus, when Martha Custis began a new courtship a few months after her husband's demise, few deemed it as inappropriate. Indeed, her suitor was an eligible, handsome young army officer named George Washington who had already seen military action in the French and Indian War. He was now in command of a force of the Virginia state militia defending frontier settlements from attack.

The couple married in 1759 and Washington moved his new family to his Mount Vernon estate located along the western bank of the Potomac River. Once settled, Washington filed papers in the local court to become the legal guardian of both of Martha's children, and he provided generously thereafter for their welfare.

The succeeding years were ones of political turmoil in the American colonies as significant economic and philosophical disputes with Great Britain periodically erupted into bloodshed. As the colonies approached independence, George Washington, a well-respected member of the Virginia gentry, served in the House of Burgesses. Later, he was appointed by the Continental Congress to command the colonial army created to oppose the major British forces being sent to America to quell the rebellion.

On the eve of the Revolution, Washington's stepson, John Parke Custis, married Eleanor Calvert and began to investigate local properties for a possible plantation of his own. In 1778, with Washington's approval, Custis purchased an 1,100-acre estate from Gerald Alexander for 1,100 pounds in Virginia currency. The tract was undeveloped but its wooded lands and excellent location along the Potomac seemed to be ideal for development at the conclusion of the Revolutionary War.

John Custis, at the age of 26, asked his stepfather's permission to enlist in the Continental Army during the crucial campaigns of 1781. Appointed to Washington's personal staff, Custis was at Yorktown in October when the British army under Lord Cornwallis was finally cornered by a combined French and American force. He became seriously ill with "camp fever" during the siege, but despite his frail health, insisted on watching the final surrender ceremonies of the British forces.

Custis was taken to Eltham to recuperate from his illness. A few weeks later, his condition deteriorated and his family was summoned to his bedside. General Washington later recounted, "I arrived [on November 5th]…in time to see poor Custis breathe his last." In a subsequent letter, Washington confided to a friend that, "Mr. Custis' death has given much distress in this family" and that, "Poor Mrs. Washington…has met with a most severe stroke in the loss of her amiable Son."

John Parke Custis was survived by his wife and two infant children, George Washington Parke and Nelly. The children were brought to Mount Vernon to be raised under the guidance of their grandparents.

George Washington Parke Custis, affectionately known to family members as "Little Washington," was eventually sent to the College of Philadelphia to complete his formal education. A lackluster student, he failed to graduate from the institution. He was later enrolled at both Princeton and Annapolis Colleges without ever completing his studies. Indeed, George Washington, then serving as President of the new republic, was distressed over his grandson's languid scholarship and was disheartened to receive a letter from one of Custis' advisors:

> If you…could by indirect means discover the state of Washington Custis's mind, it would be to be wished. He appears to me to be moped and stupid, says nothing, and is always in some hole or corner excluded from the company. Before he left Annapolis he wrote to me, desiring to know whether or not he was to return there. I answered that I was astonished at the question, and that it appeared that nothing that could be said to him had the least effect. Whether this by thwarting his views is the cause of his present behavior I know not.

To the disappointment of the family, Washington Custis returned to Mount Vernon in 1798 having miserably failed in his studies and apparently facing a dismal future. Washington formally wrote to his prodigal grandson an

An early view of the nation's capital from Arlington House, 1838.

extensive letter outlining what was expected of him while at the estate, detailing his hourly and daily responsibilities. Washington went on to advise "…the hours allotted for study, if really applied to it, instead of running up & down stairs, & wasted in conversation with any one who will talk with you, will enable you to make considerable progress in whatsoever line is marked out for you: and that you may do it, is my sincere wish."

The next year, George Washington died at home after a brief illness. His beloved wife, Martha, followed him in death just three years later. Upon his grandmother's demise, Washington Custis inherited his father's 1,100-acre Potomac plantation which had been held in trust for him. He also inherited many priceless heirlooms from his grandparents' Mount Vernon estate.

Custis began to develop his new land holdings and, in honor of his grandfather, called the property "Mount Washington." Eventually, to avoid confusion with the numerous other "Washingtons" that appeared throughout the states in the aftermath of the first President's demise, the estate was renamed Arlington after the ancestral land holdings of the Custis family on the eastern shore of Virginia.

Washington Custis commissioned the renowned architect, George Hadfield, who had worked on the construction of the United States Capitol, to assist in designing the plantation's manor house. Using the classical-revival style that was then popular throughout the United States and which dominated the architecture of the nation's capital, the mansion was modeled after the Temple of Theseus in Athens. For financial reasons, the wings of the house were constructed first. The entire building process extended over two decades.

Known formally as Arlington House, the mansion was located along the heights that overlooked the burgeoning federal city of Washington, D.C. The Arlington mansion was described in a book published in 1859:

> [Custis] commenced the erection of a beautiful mansion at Arlington, an estate of a thousand acres, left him by his father, and lying upon the west side of the Potomac, opposite Washington city...It is a most lovely spot, overlooking the Potomac; and from the noble portico, that adorns its front, so conspicuous from every point of the federal city and its vicinity, he saw that city grow into its present grand proportions, from a humble and uninteresting village.

In 1804, Custis married "Molly" Lee Fitzhugh and the couple soon moved into the newly completed north wing of the Arlington House mansion. Their only child, Mary Anna Randolph, was born there in 1808.

During this period, the Arlington estate was an active farm with the fertile fields closest to the Potomac River used for crops, an orchard, and large grazing areas for the plantation's renowned sheep herds. Early on, Custis began to hold an annual festival, the Arlington Sheep Shearing, which brought local farmers together at the estate to compete in various agriculturally related contests. The highlight of the festivities was an elaborate dinner hosted by Custis at which the local farmers were, "...[invited] to dine with him under a range of tents, one of which belonged to the illustrious Washington."

In 1812, Great Britain and the United States once again were at war. The American people, however, were deeply divided over the advisability of the war with members of the dwindling Federalist Party who were the most vocal opponents to the policies of President James Madison. Custis, a devout Federalist, became an outspoken critic of the war, claiming that it was ill advised and unnecessary. Indeed, American independence was at risk since it was quite conceivable that the United States could lose such a conflict. At the onset of the hostilities, the nation possessed an infinitesimal standing army of only 6,700 men and had just 16 naval vessels compared to a mighty British armada of over 600 warships.

In Baltimore, a group of pro-war agitators rioted and attacked the offices of the Federalist Republican, a leading opposition newspaper whose editor, Alexander Hanson, had repeatedly denounced the was as "unnecessary, inexpedient." In late July 1812, responding to the assault against the paper, several Revolutionary War veterans, including Generals "Light Horse Harry" Lee [the father of Robert E. Lee] and James McCubbin Lingan, arrived in the city to decry the mob's blatant disregard for the First Amendment and to denounce the war. At a staged rally, Lingan, Lee, and other Federalists were arrested by local militia members for haranguing the gathered crowd. On July 28, a large mob stormed the jail, taunting the imprisoned Federalists with shouts of "Tory." Furious over the impugning of his patriotism, Lingan stripped off his shirt to reveal an ugly scar he had sustained during the Revolution from a Hessian bayonet and shouted to the crowd, "Does this look like I am a traitor?" His action seemed only to inflame the already hostile mob, and Lingan and the other prisoners were repeatedly beaten. The old Revolutionary War general died as a result of the injuries he received.

In an effort to reduce tensions, Lingan's funeral was conducted privately in Georgetown, but the Federalists refused to ignore the martyrdom. (He was subsequently reinterred to Arlington National Cemetery in 1908.) Throughout Washington, poignant eulogies were offered coupled with ample denunciations of the war and President Madison. Washington Custis used the occasion to deliver one of the most eloquent funeral orations, which was eventually printed in pamphlet form for wider distribution. Custis was lauded as "…possess[ing] the fire of Demosthenes, and his actions the grace of Cicero." His eulogy was said to have made "Old warriors, who had almost forgotten how to weep, [feel] the stream of sympathy stealing down their furrowed cheeks."

In 1814, with the outcome of the war still in grave doubt, General Robert Ross landed a major force of 4,500 British regulars south of Washington, D.C. Many old Federalists, despite their opposition to the war, volunteered to defend the city from the impending British assault.

Custis manned an artillery battery during the ensuing battle, but the well-trained and heavily armed British force routed the inexperienced Americans. With the remnants of the American militia, Custis was forced to join a humiliating and disorganized retreat. Later that evening, Custis returned in despair to Arlington and watched the British destruction of Washington, including the burning of its proud symbols of the new republic – the White House and the Capitol.

When the War of 1812 was concluded shortly thereafter, the nation once again turned its attention toward domestic pursuits. Slavery remained the most obvious contradiction to America's republican ideals. It was opposed by most educated Americans and seen as a national (not sectional) problem that had to be jointly resolved. Well-meaning Southerners cooperated with their Northern counterparts in seeking alternative labor sources and a way to abolish the system.

Although he owned 60 slaves, Washington Custis became one of Virginia's leading opponents of slavery, calling it "…the mightiest serpent that ever infested the world." Custis even allowed his slaves a limited education and incorporated into his will a provision that required the manumission of all of Arlington's slaves within five years of his death. This mandate was destined to become irrelevant with the onset of the Civil War in 1861.

Members of the U.S. Signal Corps posing next to the graves of Washington and Molly Custis, 1864. Recent burials of Union soldiers are apparent in the background.

In 1817, the "American Society for Colonizing the Free People of Colour of the United States" was formed to encourage the emancipation of slaves and the deportation of the freed men to the northern African colony of Liberia. Custis joined such notables as Henry Clay, John Randolph, Daniel Webster, and James Madison in supporting the society's efforts; chapters were eventually established in all of the states with the notable exception of South Carolina. However, even with the modest financial support of the federal government, the American Colonization Society's approach to the nation's insidious institution proved impractical since the vast majority of slaves were American born and birth rates far exceeded emigration. As a result, slavery continued to flourish throughout the cotton south.

In 1824, the nation welcomed the return of the Marquis de Lafayette to the United States for a triumphal farewell tour of America. For most Americans, the Marquis remained the embodiment of the ideals of the American Revolution. His visit was widely celebrated throughout the country with innumerable galas and celebrations held in his honor. In October, Lafayette arrived in Washington, D.C., en route to special ceremonies being conducted in Yorktown for the 43rd anniversary of the British surrender. On the outskirts of Washington, Lafayette was met by an official delegation that included Washington Custis. His carriage was escorted to the center of the city for extensive welcoming ceremonies. After a formal dinner in his honor at the White House hosted by President James Monroe, Lafayette "...paid a private visit to the family of MR. CUSTIS of Arlington." While at the estate, the two distinguished gentlemen freely shared memories of George Washington with Lafayette openly reminiscing about his role in the American Revolution.

Two years later, Custis published a series of articles entitled, "Conversations with Lafayette," which were syndicated in both the Alexandria Gazette and the National Intelligencer. The articles contained detailed accounts of the Marquis' experiences in the American war for independence and recounted his close, personal friendship with George Washington. During this period, Custis also began to compose modest dramas focusing on historical American events, themes, and settings. Although several of Custis' plays were performed throughout the eastern states and enjoyed moderate popularity, most were undistinguished in terms of literary merit.

Custis was also an amateur painter. His canvases depicted Revolutionary War battle scenes centering around the heroic figure of his grandfather. Six of Custis' paintings are known to exist – the battles of Trenton, Princeton, Germantown, and Monmouth; Washington at Yorktown; and Cornwallis' Surrender at Yorktown.

In 1831, Mary Anna Randolph, the sole offspring of Washington and Molly Custis, began to receive the romantic attentions of a young Army officer and recent West Point graduate, Robert E. Lee. Although the Lee lineage was distinguished, Custis initially did not approve of his daughter's suitor or courtship. Indeed, the Lee family had suffered a series of well-publicized and embarrassing financial reversals. The patriarch of the Arlington estate feared that the young Lieutenant Lee would be unable to provide adequately for his beloved Mary, reducing her to a hard life as the wife of a lower grade Army officer on a meager government salary.

As Lee became a frequent visitor to Arlington, through his personal charm and stellar character, he gradually won the approval of Washington Custis and on June 30, 1831, Mary Randolph Custis and Robert E. Lee were married in the drawing room of the Arlington House mansion. The event was briefly noted in the National Intelligencer, "Marriage: At Arlington House, by the Rev. Dr. Keith, Lieut. ROBERT LEE, of the U. States Corps of Engineers, to Miss MARY A.R. CUSTIS, only daughter of G.W.P. CUSTIS, Esq."

The ceremony was marred by a heavy summer rainstorm which delayed the arrival of the minister. Marietta Turner, a member of the wedding party and a Custis relative, later recounted the humorous arrival of the Reverend Keith:

> The night of the wedding at Arlington happened to be one of steady rain, and much fun arose from the appearance of the Reverend Ruel Keith, who arrived drenched to the skin and though a tall man, was compelled to conduct the nuptial service in the clothes of my cousin, George Washington Parke Custis, a very great gentleman but a very small man so far as

inches were concerned.

After a week's repose at Arlington, the newlyweds moved to Lee's duty station at Fort Monroe, Virginia. There the couple made their home for a brief period. As it became apparent that Lee's military career would necessitate prolonged absences from home, it was agreed that Mary should return to her Arlington home. Over the next several years, six of the seven Lee children were born on the estate.

In 1848, after Lee had returned from the Mexican War as a Brevet Colonel for a brief tour of duty in Washington, Custis was asked to participate in Independence Day ceremonies that would mark the beginning of construction of the Washington Monument. As the last surviving link to the first President, Custis' brief speech honoring his grandfather was an integral part of the festivities. Construction on the 550-foot monument continued until the onset of the Civil War, but the structure remained unfinished and would not be completed during Custis' lifetime.

In May 1853, tragedy struck Arlington with the death of Custis' beloved wife, Molly. She was buried in the small family plot located in a densely wooded area a short distance from the Arlington House mansion. Deeply distraught over the loss of his wife, Custis survived for only another 4 years and died on October 10, 1857. At his behest, the patriarch of the Arlington estate was interred beside his wife. The National Intelligencer eulogized:

> It becomes our painful duty to announce the decease of the venerable GEORGE WASHINGTON PARKE CUSTIS, the last of the members of the family of WASHINGTON.
>
> MR. CUSTIS died at Arlington, near this city after a brief illness, on the morning of the 10th instant, in the 77th year of his age…Thousands from this country and from foreign lands who have visited Arlington to commune with our departed friend, and look upon the touching memorials there treasured up with care of him who was first in the hearts of his countrymen, will not forget the charm thrown over all by the ease, grace, interest, and vivacity of manners and conversation of him whose voice alas! is silent now. The multitudes of our fellow-citizens accustomed, in the heat of summer, to resort to the shades of Arlington will hereafter miss that old man eloquent, who ever extended to them a warm-hearted welcome and became partaker of their joy.
>
> It becomes our painful duty to announce the decease of the venerable GEORGE WASHINGTON PARKE CUSTIS, the last of the members of the family of WASHINGTON.

CHAPTER THREE

Your Old Home Has . . . Been Desecrated

—*Robert E. Lee*

With the death of his father-in-law in 1857, Colonel Robert E. Lee returned to Arlington and assumed the day-to-day operations of the plantation. In the ensuing years, sectional strife between the North and South intensified, culminating in the secession of seven Southern states in early 1861. The Lees were dismayed by the news and still hoped for some reconciliation. Mary Custis Lee wrote to a friend in February:

> ...we have changed our Post Office new to Arlington near Washington, D.C. I am so much obliged to you for thinking of us in these trouble[ed] times...Has all care for and pride in their Country died [in] the South that they are willing to tear her in pieces and...to see her glorious flag trailing in the dust[?]...we have lived and fought and prospered under this flag so many years and tho' the South has suffered much from the meddling of Northern fanatics, yet do they expect to have better; are there no rights & privileges but those of negro slavery?...we in the border states are so much annoyed that our slaves have become almost useless. In our own family we have lost numbers who have been decoyed off after my Father's death. We were preserved from [our] out break excited by two abolitionists who were constantly over here as we learned afterwards, one of whom I am happy to say is new in the penitentiary for 14 years. We were preserved I say by the special mercy of God. The *Tribune & New York Times* published the most villainous attacks upon my husband by name and upon my Father's memory in language I would not pollute my lips by repeating and yet after all these wrongs, I would lay down my life could I save our 'Union.'...I pray now that [God] will preserve us from Civil War.

Like many southerners, Lee had dual loyalties—first to his state and then to his country. He sincerely hoped that his beloved Virginia would remain within the Union despite the election of Abraham Lincoln to the presidency. Such delusions, however, were irrevocably shattered on April 17, 1861, when the Richmond legislature withdrew Virginia's ratification of the United States Constitution, effectively linking the Old Dominion's fate to that of the infant Confederacy. Rather than bear arms against his native state, Lee instead chose to resign his federal commission. He left Arlington on April 22, 1861, to offer his services to the Virginia militia. Later, Lee commented, "...a Union that can only be maintained by sword and bayonets ... has no charm for me." Mary Lee remained temporarily behind at Arlington in a futile attempt to maintain normalcy, but events soon conspired against her and forced her to flee the estate.

Across the Potomac, General Winfield Scott, the elderly commander of the Union Army, knew well the strategic importance of Lee's Arlington plantation. Indeed, with its breathtaking view of Washington, the ridges of Arlington Heights could be easily fortified by the Confederate Army with long and medium-range artillery, thereby placing virtually every federal agency and institution in jeopardy. Rather than allow such an eventuality, Scott ordered federal forces to seize the estate.

On the night of May 23, 1861, in the first major military action of the Civil War, 14,000 Union troops quietly crossed the Potomac River by way of the Long and Aqueduct Bridges (the current sites of the 14th Street and Key Bridges) and occupied Arlington. They simultaneously captured the neighboring port city of Alexandria. This uncontested troop movement was accomplished at the cost of only a single casualty, Col. Elmer Ellsworth. He had been shot and mortally wounded by the proprietor of the Marshall House Inn for

Arlington House under Union occupation. The Lee estate was seized by the U.S. Army in May 1861 to prevent Confederate fortification of the plantation's strategic ridges.

removing the establishment's Confederate flag.

With Arlington now firmly under Union occupation, General Irvin McDowell converted the estate's manor house into a comfortable headquarters for the Army of the Potomac. P. Regis de Tribriand, a French observer traveling with the Union Army observed: "The tents of the guard and of the servants of the staff were set up in the gardens, trampled by men and animals. The park roads were deeply furrowed by the continual passage of artillery and ammunition wagons everywhere." Radical alterations of the grounds were soon ordered, including the hasty construction of two defensive forts—Whipple and McPherson—as part of the growing defensive perimeter protecting Washington, D.C., from Confederate attack. Upon hearing of the loss of his property and the subsequent Union actions, in a letter to his daughters, Lee lamented, "Your old home has been so desecrated that I cannot bear to think of it. I should have preferred it to have been wiped from this earth, its beautiful hill sunk, and its sacred trees buried rather than have been degraded…" In a subsequent letter, he mused about the possibility of purchasing his boyhood home in Westmoreland County: "I am much pleased at your description of Stratford & your visit. It is endeared to me by many recollections & it has always been a great desire of my life to be able to purchase it. Now that we have no other home & the one we so loved has been so foully polluted; the desire is stronger with me than ever."

Thousands of Union soldiers converged upon Arlington during the early months of the war. There, inexperienced officers continually drilled and trained the new recruits. In July 1861, General McDowell, pressured by the vocal demands of Northern newspapers for action, prematurely ordered his Army of Northeastern Virginia to seize the key railway junction at Manassas, some 20 miles west of the city. A major Confederate force under the command of Brigadier Generals P.G.T. Beauregard and Joe E. Johnston was engaged there. During the ensuing day-long battle, federal forces were routed and forced to retreat in disorder toward Washington. The escaping soldiers were later regrouped only after they reached the relative safety of the new Union fortifications along Arlington Heights.

The disastrous defeat necessitated a change in military command. General McDowell was replaced by the young, brash George McClellan who was entrusted with the monumental task of rejuvenating the dispirited federal Army. McClellan immediately moved into the Arlington House mansion for the winter of 1861-62 and began preparations for the spring campaign season.

In late March 1862, McClellan ferried his reorganized Army of the Potomac to southeastern Virginia in a bold and daring effort to capture Richmond in a surprise attack from the east. President Lincoln, however, ordered that a portion of the Union army remain behind in the vicinity of the capital, including the defensive fortifications at Arlington, to protect it from a possible Confederate counter-offensive. During McClellan's painfully slow advance up the Virginia peninsula, the Confederate Commander, Joe E. Johnston, was severely wounded outside of Richmond at the Battle of Seven Pines and was replaced by General Robert E. Lee who successfully defended the Confederate capital and forced a federal retreat.

Arlington's function as a major Army headquarters was soon discontinued as the war shifted away from Northern Virginia. Several lower ranking officers moved into the vacant mansion to coordinate the capital's western defenses. Since the war remained relatively distant, many elaborate galas and balls were staged at Arlington House to provide a diversion for the officers who no doubt enjoyed the irony of hosting these events in the home of the now Confederate Commander. The hundreds of less fortunate enlisted men still stationed in the neighboring forts and camps along Arlington Heights were forced to content themselves with foraging around the Lee estate for materials that would help make their lives more bearable. During this time, the land was denuded of small trees and underbrush while fences were torn down to provide an ample supply of wood for camp fires and the construction of rifle pits. The excellent stable facilities at Arlington were in constant use by the federal cavalry to quarter their horses. The estate also served as a convenient staging area for periodic excursions deep into hostile Virginia. Yet the chance for actual combat seemed remote as one Union soldier stationed at Camp Leslie along Arlington Heights lamented in a letter home: "I have not ben so fortuneate to mett any Rebels yet and maby I wont but I sill like soldering."

The Arlington House Mansion had become a major sightseeing attraction for the many Washington residents who were anxious to glimpse the antebellum home of the now legendary Confederate Commander of the Army of Northern Virginia, Robert E. Lee. Even President Lincoln made an occasional visit to the grounds to escape the awesome burdens of his office and to enjoy the solitude of the plantation with its panoramic vista of Washington, D.C.

The Arlington Burial Ground

In 1862, the United States Congress passed "An Act for the Collection of Taxes in the Insurrectionary Districts," which levied property taxes on land under Confederate occupation. Under the provisions of the legislation, a tax of $92.07 was assessed on the Arlington plantation. Informed of this situation in 1864, Mrs. Lee, now totally an invalid and confined to a wheelchair, attempted to comply with the law's provisions by sending designated representatives to Union-occupied Alexandria to offer payment. The federal tax commissioners stationed in the city refused to accept these funds on the dubious legal grounds that the property owners had to appear personally. Shortly thereafter, Arlington was officially confiscated for tax default and the property was sold at auction to the United States government for a mere $26,800.

That same year, the War Department began to assess the suitability of federal properties as potential burial grounds since the government had been

National Archives

The Field of the Dead (Section 13). Over 16,000 Union soldiers were buried near the Arlington House mansion to prevent the Lees from ever returning to their antebellum home. These original grave markers were made of wood.

under severe criticism for the seemingly callous way gallant federal soldiers had been interred in remote and austere locations. With the demand for adequate grave space for the seemingly endless stream of Civil War casualties at a peak, the Arlington estate seemed an ideal location for a new federal cemetery with its beautiful setting and large acreage.

On May 13, 1864, a small burial party was ordered to the west bank of the Potomac River near the northeastern boundary of the Lee plantation. There, they interred a hapless new recruit, Private William Christman, 67th Pennsylvania Infantry. Christman, just 21 years at the time of his death, had enlisted in the army just two months earlier and had spent the majority of his brief military career confined to Lincoln Hospital in a losing battle against peritonitis. His burial on the Lee plantation was near the site of a small cemetery reserved for the plantation's slaves and was notable as the first military funeral on land that would eventually encompass Arlington National Cemetery.

For the next few weeks, burials continued in this remote section of the Lee estate, but several staff officers stationed on the plantation were opposed to the use of General Lee's estate for burials and argued against any further expansion of grave facilities. The Quartermaster General of the Army, Montgomery Meigs, the individual charged with the administration of federal cemeteries, however, was angry and embittered over what he perceived to be Lee's treasonable behavior. He requested permission from Secretary of War Edwin Stanton to formally designate 200 acres in the immediate vicinity of

A letter from G. McCord who was stationed at Camp Leslie located on Arlington Heights. McCord writes, "I have not ben so fortunate to mett any Rebels."

the Arlington House mansion as a national cemetery and to encircle the residence with graves effectively making it unsuitable for private habitation. On June 15, 1864, orders were formally issued to set aside "The Arlington Mansion and the grounds immediately surrounding it...for a Military Cemetery. The bodies of all soldiers dying in the Hospitals of the vicinity of Washington and Alexandria...will be interred in this Cemetery." The same day that the cemetery was commissioned, 65 burials took place on the property including several in the area that encompassed Mrs. Lee's rose garden. By the end of 1864, the graves of over 7,000 Union soldiers located in what was popularly known as the "Field of the Dead" (Section 13) scarred the once beautiful landscape and rows of crude, wooden, plank markers stretched to the horizon.

The military burials at Arlington were frequently conducted without ceremony or religious services. Quartermaster General Meigs notified the Secretary of War:

> I find that soldiers buried at the military cemeteries in this District are generally interred without any religious ceremony. On inquiry yesterday of the workmen engaged in digging graves where forty soldiers are interred daily, they informed me that they had seldom seen a chaplain at a funeral. Some of them thought none had been there for three weeks. It is impossible for the chaplains of hospitals to accompany each body to the grave. It is a daily duty, and the chaplains' whole time would be taken up in its performance. The Quartermaster's Department is, I think, unjustly blamed for interring the soldiers without appropriate ceremonies. It has not the appointment or employment of chaplains. Its officers are occupied with their appropriate duties, and cannot be present at the cemetery constantly. The interments are going on all day. If from the chaplains attached to the many hospitals of this District one could be detailed daily to be on duty during the whole day at each of the military cemeteries now in use – one at Arlington, the other at Alexandria – it would give great satisfaction to the friends of our soldiers. The chaplain on duty should remain constantly at the cemetery until relieved by his successor. The interments could be made at certain hours two or three times a day, the bodies being deposited at the side of the graves, which are prepared beforehand, and the service could be thus performed over several bodies at a time. If this cannot be done, the only substitute which occurs to me as possible will be the employment by the Quartermaster's Department of an ordained minister at a sufficient salary as a guardian or custodian of each cemetery, making it a part of the contract with him that he shall live at the cemetery in quarters

to be prepared for him, take charge of the whole conduct of interments, and perform appropriate religious services over all persons interred therein. I think that the detail by military authority of a chaplain to this duty daily is the better and more appropriate mode of meeting the difficulty, and I only suggest the employment by the Quartermaster's Department of persons for this purpose as a last resort.

The grave of Lt. John Rodgers Meigs located in Section 1 just a short distance from the Custis-Lee Mansion. Meigs was killed in the Shenandoah Valley in 1864 and was the son of the Quartermaster General who established Arlington National Cemetery.

With a cessation of hostilities in 1865, General Lee settled in Lexington, Virginia, where he assumed the presidency of Washington College. His wife remained bitter over the loss of her ancestral home and in 1866 wrote to a friend, "I learn that my garden laid out with so much taste by my dear father's own hands has all been changed, the splendid forest levelled to the ground, the small enclosure allotted to his and my mother's remains surrounded closely by the graves of those who aided to bring all this ruin on the children and country. They are even planted up to the very door without any regard to common decency." In another letter she elaborated, "Even savages would have spared that place…yet they have done everything to debase and desecrate it."

General Lee quietly began to make inquires about possibly reclaiming the Arlington estate. In April, he wrote to Francis Smith, his lawyer in Alexandria:

...Cannot the property under the laws of VA. be reclaimed? I would be obliged to you if in your power to have the tax sale examined & to let me know the facts in the case; whether the Sale was regular & legal, & what can be done. I have refrained from taking any steps as to the recovery of the property as the Executor of G.W. Custis until I should see whether I would be restored to Civil rights, & have thought that any premature application on my part might prejudice the claim & perhaps induce some action of Congress unfavorable to its restoration to its rightful owners. As you are acquainted with G.W. Custis' will I need not to inform you that he left it to his daughter, Mrs. Lee during her life, & afterwards to the [grand]son. When Mrs. Lee left the place which she did on being informed that it was to be seized by the U.S. forces, she left her manager, servants, teams, Cattle etc. on the place...the use of the great body of wood, the sale of furniture, etc. etc. has surely amounted to more than the taxes.

With my kindest regards to Mrs. Smith, your family,
I am most truly,
R.E. Lee

Despite the end of battlefield casualties and ongoing legal maneuverings, Arlington's mandate as a national cemetery continued into the post-war peri- od. Cleanup operations were being conducted on virtually all major Civil War battlefields since, in the haste of conflict, thousands of soldiers had been either left unburied or interred in shallow, inadequate graves that now posed a major health problem for the surrounding communities. Near Bull Run, the bones of literally hundreds of soldiers were routinely uncovered and trans- ported to Arlington for burial. A vault was placed in a large pit dug in the Lee's rose garden to accommodate these remains in a common grave. The National Intelligencer graphically described the scene:

A more terrible spectacle can hardly be conceived than is to be seen within a dozen rods of the Arlington mansion. A circular pit, twenty feet deep and the same in diameter, has been sunk by the side of the flower garden, cemented and divided into com- partments, and down into this gloomy receptacle are cast the bones of such soldiers as perished on the field and either were not buried at all or were so covered up as to have their bones mingle indiscriminately together. At the time we looked into this gloomy cavern, a literal Golgotha, there were piled together skulls in one division, legs in another, arms in another, and ribs in another, what were estimated as the bones of two thousand human beings. They were dropping fragmentary skeletons into this receptacle almost daily.

The vault was filled and sealed in September 1866, and a granite monument was placed above it to commemorate the fallen soldiers. The inscription on the sarcophagus reads:

> Beneath this stone repose the bones of two
> thousand one hundred and eleven unknown soldiers,
> gathered after the war from the fields of Bull Run
> and the route to the Rappahannock. Their remains could
> not be identified, but their names and deaths are
> recorded in the archives of their country, and its grateful
> citizens honor them as of their noble army of martyrs.
> May they rest in peace.

Most northerners agreed with the government's confiscation of the Lee estate and its conversion to a national cemetery. The Morning Chronicle called the creation of the Arlington Burial Ground, "A righteous use of the estate of the rebel General Lee," and charged him with the "[...murder of] hundreds of Union heroes." Still, a few individuals were distressed over what they perceived to be a vengeful act. One visitor to Arlington after the Civil War wrote:

> We found ourselves at Arlington House looking back across the Potomac at the glorious view of the distant city. The house is placed in a lovely situation on the crest of a beautifully wooded slope. It is a queer old fashion place, with heavy columns and flights of steps, strangely like what it is being now turned into – a mausoleum. In front workmen were busy restoring the outer wall for the park has become enclosed as a cemetery. To see the home of Robert Lee sacked and made into a cemetery, and to fancy the thoughts that would fill the great heart were so strange to me, and in their strangeness so painful, that I doubt whether I ever had a sadder walk than the visit to the heights of Arlington.

Robert E. Lee died in 1870 without ever returning to Arlington. He was buried in the chapel of Washington College, which later, in his honor, changed its name to Washington and Lee University. Mary Custis Lee, however, did make one brief and sad pilgrimage to Arlington in 1873 to visit some of her former servants who remained on the estate now in the employ of the United States government. Upon arrival, surrounded by the thousands of graves of "enemy" soldiers, Mary Lee was so distraught that she refused to leave her carriage. In utter despair, deprived now of both her devoted husband and her beloved Arlington, she returned to Lexington where she survived for only another five months.

In accordance with the original will of Washington Custis, claim to Arlington now fell to his eldest grandson and namesake, George Washington Custis Lee. Lee, desirous of claiming his inheritance, asked the United States Congress to recognize his rightful ownership of the Arlington property, but the legislators rejected all of his appeals. Advised by his lawyers that his sole recourse was to take legal action, Custis Lee filed suit in the Circuit Court of Alexandria in April 1877 demanding eviction of the federal government from the estate as a trespasser.

The lower court ruled in favor of Lee and ordered the federal government to vacate the property and restore it to its antebellum appearance. Faced with the monumental and unpleasant task of disinterring over 16,000 soldiers, the government filed an appeal with the United States Supreme Court in 1882. In George Washington Custis Lee v. the United States of America the court, in a five-to-four decision, concurred with the earlier verdict and upheld Lee's claim to Arlington.

Representatives of the government, with all legal recourse exhausted, finally entered into serious negotiations with Custis Lee for the formal purchase of the Arlington estate. Lee agreed to sell the property for $150,000, a fee Congress gladly appropriated in March 1883. Title to the property was officially transferred to the United States on April 24, 1883, forever ensuring Arlington's mandate as a national cemetery.

Post-War Arlington

During the early years of Arlington's existence as a national cemetery, landscaping practices were often primitive and unpredictable. Grave markers were still constructed out of wood with the names of the soldiers merely painted on. The ravages of time and weather required replacement on a regular five-year cycle at a cost to the government of $1.24 each.

Quartermaster General Montgomery Meigs began to investigate alternative, more enduring grave markers in hopes of reducing government expense. At his order, an experimental stone composed of a metal alloy was placed in Section 13. Although this marker proved durable and still remains, the federal government instead adopted in 1872 the more traditional and aesthetically pleasing white marble for use in all of its national cemeteries. By 1880, rows of new, gleaming white standardized gravestones were evident throughout the Arlington Burial Ground.

Uniform stones were required in all enlisted areas at Arlington, but in Section 1, the so-called "Officer's Section," cemetery regulations allowed for more decorative stones, limited in size and scope only by a family's personal wealth and imagination. This caused what some critics termed as "riotous conditions" with a vast array of unique funeral architecture erected in elaborate efforts to memorialize the lives of the deceased. Major General Wallace Fitz Randolph, an artilleryman, even had an actual cannon placed over his grave upon his death in 1910 to serve as his memorial. Allegedly, he claimed that he had spent a lifetime behind an artillery piece so he now preferred to spend an eternity under one.

The grave marker of Lieutenant John Rodgers Meigs, the son of the Quartermaster General and the founder of the cemetery, is also unusual. Lieutenant Meigs served with the Army of the Shenandoah under the command of Philip Sheridan in 1864. In October, near Harrisonburg, Virginia, Meigs carelessly approached three unidentified horsemen who he mistakenly believed to be local civilians. In fact, they were Confederate cavalrymen wearing rain gear that had partially obscured their uniforms. Realizing his mistake too late, Meigs was mortally wounded in a hail of gunfire.

General Sheridan notified the Quartermaster General of his son's demise and added that the Lieutenant had been killed "without resistance of any kind," implying that he had been murdered by Confederate partisans wearing civilian garb. General Meigs commissioned a poignant monument to his son depicting the young soldier in full military uniform lying prostrate on the ground surrounded by hoof prints, his revolver at his side. The marker remains a sad reminder of a tragedy in the Shenandoah Valley a century ago.

Although Arlington was primarily designed for the interment of federal soldiers, many Confederate prisoners had died in local hospitals during the war and required appropriate military funerals. The cemetery's original burial records show that all such interments were designated with the derogatory term, "REBEL," and indicate that the first southern soldier buried at Arlington was an unknown Confederate interred on May 20, 1864. Shortly thereafter, on May 30, the first identifiable Confederate, Levi Reinhardt, 23rd North Carolina Regiment, was buried after his death at Carver Hospital.

After the end of the Civil War, Reinhardt and the remains of many other southern soldiers were reclaimed by family members and returned to their native states for appropriate burial. Those Confederate soldiers who remained at Arlington were denied grave decorations and excluded from all post-war memorial tributes. Only after the passage of time had ameliorated the intense passions of the conflict was it decided to acknowledge the southern soldiers still buried at Arlington. In 1906, Congress formally authorized the construction of a Confederate memorial in the cemetery.

The Freedmen's Village

The Freedmen's Bureau under the direction of General O. O. Howard was created in 1865 to look after the welfare of the slaves newly emancipated by the XIII Amendment. A freedmen's village was established on the grounds of the former Lee plantation and flourished, eventually consisted of over 100

An early map of the Freedman's Village that was established on the cemetery grounds in 1865. Over 3,800 former slaves are interred at Arlington; their headstones are marked with the inscription "citizen" or "civilian."

homes housing 1,000 people. The African-Americans who lived on the estate were taught trades, skills, and reading. Harper's Weekly described the village, "…[as] quite lively, having a large number of children in it. For these there is a school house; there is, besides, a home for the aged, a hospital, church, tailor and other work-shops, with other public buildings. The principal street is over a quarter of a mile long, and the place presents a clean and prosperous appearance at all times." A contemporary guidebook of Washington, D.C., however, was more critical. It claimed:

> [Arlington Village] is one of the various settlements established by the Government to relieve the Capital form being overflowed by the freedmen…the village is in the charge of the Freemen's Bureau, and is in better condition than the majority of such establishments throughout the country, so that it cannot be justly regarded as a fair specimen of them. The officers of the Bureau have, frequently, hard work to keep the Negroes in subjection, and to enforce their orders. Once or twice it has been necessary to summon the aid of the military…it would seem [appropriate]

to abandon it as soon as possible, and thus relieve the country of the heavy load of taxation which its support renders necessary.

The Freedmen's Bureau was abolished in 1872, but the Arlington Village remained in existence until the late 1890s when it was finally razed to make way for further cemetery expansion.

Arlington Cemetery ultimately became the final resting place for over 3,800 former slaves. Most are interred in Section 27, which was traditionally known as the "Contraband" section. The colloquial term, "contraband," was used in the 19th Century in reference to runaway slaves and was said to have originated with General Benjamin Franklin Butler, the colorful and contentious commander of Fort Monroe. At the onset of the Civil War, several slaves fled their tidewater plantations to seek refuge within the confines of the fort. Butler, exceeding his authority and violating stated administration policy, refused to return the black refugees to their owners claiming that he would, "Hold these Negroes as contraband of war…[since they are] capable of being used for warlike purposes."

Throughout the Civil War, thousands of slaves continually crossed federal lines into freedom. Many settled in the vicinity of Washington, D.C. Forced to live in cramped quarters with unsanitary conditions, many of these former slaves died from disease and were buried at Arlington in Sections 23 and 27. Their grave markers were designated simply with the inscription, "Civilian" or "Citizen." Interspersed among these stones are the graves of numerous African-American soldiers who served in the Union army during the Civil War or with federal forces in subsequent American conflicts before the integration of the Armed Forces. Their graves bear the abbreviation U.S.C.T. for United States Colored Troops. Three of these soldiers received the nation's highest award for valor, the Medal of Honor.

The First Memorial Day

In 1868, as Arlington's size swelled with the continuing burial of Civil War veterans, General John Alexander Logan issued General Order #11 that created Decoration Day, a time for the nation to pause to honor deceased veterans. The order read in part:

> The 30th day of May, 1868, is designated for the purpose of strewing with flowers, or otherwise decorating the graves of comrades who died in defense of their country during the late rebellion…We should guard their graves with sacred vigilance…Let no neglect, no ravages of time, testify to the present or to the coming generations that we have forgotten as a people the cost of a free and undivided republic…Let us, then, at the time appointed, gather around their sacred remains, and garland the passionless mounds above them with the choicest flowers of springtime; let us raise above them the dear old flag they saved; let us in this solemn presence renew our pledge to aid

and to assist those whom have left among us a sacred charge upon the Nation's gratitude – the soldier's and sailor's widow and orphan.

In keeping with the spirit of Logan's order, the first commemorative celebrations were conducted at the Arlington House mansion and were attended by Generals Ulysses Grant and James Garfield, both future presidents. A contemporary account in the *New York Times* described the festivities:

The ceremonies consequent upon the decoration of the soldiers' graves at the Arlington National Cemetery were most imposing and impressive. About 10:30 o'clock the Committee completed their labors, and four large army wagons were filled with evergreens of every description, and the Committee of Arrangements, accompanied by the ladies who assisted in preparing the flowers, proceeded to Arlington Heights in carriages, omnibuses and ambulances, via the Long Bridge. Upon their arrival at Arlington, the flowers and evergreens were turned over to the Decoration Committee, who took charge of them until the time arrived for the decoration of the grounds. About the same hour throngs of people, in every manner of vehicle, from gorgeous private equipages, with liveried coachmen and outriders, and public carriages to the more modest rockaways of humble citizens, started for the grounds. Some idea of the immense crowd may be formed from the fact that more than three hundred vehicles passed the Arlington toll gate en route to the cemetery, and it is estimated that at least five thousand pedestrians were present. The day was propitious, although somewhat too warm for comfort, but nevertheless the prearranged program was carried out without variation.

GEN. GARFIELD, of Ohio, delivered the address...The most impressive feature in the ceremonies was the procession of the children of the Soldiers' and Sailors' Orphan Asylum, in charge of the officers and managers of the Association, and Committee on Decorations, followed by friends generally. As the procession moved around the garden south of the mansion, the children strewed flowers upon the graves along the line of march, and halted at the tomb of the unknown soldiers who fell in Virginia from Bull Run to the Rappahannock during the early years of the war. The monument contains an inscription appropriate to their valor, and states that the dust of 2,111 soldiers is there commingled. The children, boys and girls, wearing mourning scarfs, sung a plaintive song, and during the playing of the Dead March by the Fifty Cavalry Band, the tomb was appropriately decorated amid marked solemnity, many shedding tears. Meantime a national salute was fired from the front of the Arlington House. The procession then re-formed and marched to the flag stand at the principal cemetery. There was a prayer, a hymn by eight male voices, and the reading of President LINCOLN'S dedicatory address at Gettysburg, the last named by HON. HALBERT E. PAINE, of Wisconsin, a General in the late war. The Committee on Decorations, with the orphans, then deployed and took positions at the different stands of flowers and flags, and at once proceeded to the decoration of the graves throughout the Cemetery. The bands relieved each other in playing appropriate music. The ceremonies concluded with the air of the Star-Spangled Banner, a prayer and benediction.

The popularity of the holiday increased in ensuing years and was finally declared a national holiday by formal act of Congress in 1888 and officially renamed Memorial Day. The crowds for subsequent Memorial Day services at Arlington grew so large that the limited facilities at the mansion were inadequate to accommodate all who wished to participate. Congress appropriated funds for the construction of an amphitheater to be located just south of Arlington House near the monument to the 2,111 unknown soldiers. Its planned size would be capable of accommodating up to 1,500 people. The trellised structure, completed in 1874, was described in a turn of the century guidebook: "Here art and nature have joined hands and formed one of those delightful combinations which touch the heart, and upon the hallowing velvet turf the companies who have come here upon Memorial Day have their patriotism quickened by the recital of the valorous deeds of those who died."

Civil War Notables

Among the many Civil War notables buried at Arlington, Philip Kearny was one of the most interesting. Despite failing to graduate from the West Point military academy, Kearny nonetheless was commissioned and saw action in the war with Mexico. In a daring and chivalrous cavalry charge at Churubusco, he lost as arm but won the adulation of the American commander, Winfield Scott, who called Kearny, "The bravest man I ever saw, a perfect soldier."

Kearny continued his military career after the war and traveled to Europe where he served with the French during their colonial campaigns in Algiers. He received the French Grand Cross for bravery for his actions in northern Africa and later returned to the United States where he received a command in the newly formed Army of the Potomac. He quickly earned the respect of his men and created the famed "Kearny Patch," a diamond-shaped insignia which was proudly worn by his troops on their kepis and distinguished them as members of "Fighting Phil's Red Diamond Regiment."

In 1862, after the Union army's disastrous defeat at the battle of Second Bull Run, Kearny's men engaged a major Confederate force near Chantilly, Virginia. As night approached and both lines became confused, the General mistakenly rode into a

Confederate position. Ignoring shouts to surrender, Kearny instead wheeled his horse around and attempted to escape in a hail of gunfire. Several bullets struck the General killing him instantly. His body was taken behind the Confederate lines to the headquarters of a former West Point classmate, General A.P. Hill. Hill sadly gazed upon his friend's body and lamented, "Poor Kearny, he deserved a better death than that."

When General Robert E. Lee was notified of Kearny's demise, he immediately ordered the body to be returned to the Union lines under a flag of truce. Likewise, all of Kearny's possessions, including his horse, were similarly returned. Lee later compensated the Confederate government for these captured items out of his own personal funds.

Kearny was buried near the Old Amphitheater at Arlington Cemetery; his grave is marked by one of the cemetery's two equestrian statues, a gift from the state of New Jersey in 1914.

Nearby is the grave of James Tanner, a little known corporal who played a minor but significant role in American history. Tanner patriotically enlisted in the Union Army at the age of 19 and was seriously wounded during the second battle of Bull Run in 1862. Surgeons were forced to amputate both of his legs, but Tanner was later able to walk after being fitted with two wooden prostheses. Unable to contribute further to the Union cause as an infantryman, Tanner studied stenography, a vital skill in the era of handwritten records, and eventually found employment with the War Department in Washington.

On the evening of April 14, 1865, Tanner attended a gala at Grover's Theater in Washington, D.C., celebrating Lee's surrender of the Army of Northern Virginia and the imminent end of four bloody years of combat. Midway through the festivities, word was received that President Abraham Lincoln had been shot across town at Ford's Theater. Tanner, initially believing that the report was false, attempted to calm the panicked crowd but when the rumor was confirmed, he, along with many of the other theatergoers, hurriedly made their way to 10th Street, the site of the shooting.

The President's limp body had already been carried across the street from Ford's Theater to the Peterson boarding house. His attending physicians did not believe the President could survive even a short trip back to the White House. Around midnight, Tanner volunteered to record the testimony of the many witnesses to the shooting. Throughout the remainder of the night, sitting opposite Secretary of War Edwin Stanton, Tanner took copious shorthand notes as the pursuit of the assassins was planned and organized. He later recalled that, "In fifteen minutes I had enough down to hang John Wilkes Booth." Tanner's record of the events at the Peterson boarding house became the most comprehensive and accurate account of the hours immediately after the Lincoln assassination.

Buried just a few yards from Tanner is General Arthur MacArthur, the father of General of the Army Douglas MacArthur. Arthur MacArthur served with the 24th Wisconsin during the Civil War and had a renowned military career. He received the Congressional Medal of Honor for his actions in 1863 during the

Battle of Missionary Ridge when he led his troops in a valiant charge against a strongly fortified Confederate position maintained by the Army of the Tennessee. The Union victory, resulting in part from this action, opened the way for Sherman's invasion of Georgia and his famed march to the sea which hastened the demise of the Confederate cause.

Eighty years later, MacArthur's son, Douglas, would likewise be awarded the Congressional Medal of Honor for his heroic defense of the Philippines during the Japanese assault on the islands in 1941-42. Together, they remain the only father and son recipients of the nation's highest decoration of valor.

In Section 1 just behind Arlington House is the grave of the legendary founder of the game of baseball, Abner Doubleday. He, like many Civil War officers, graduated from West Point and became a general. Stationed with the Union garrison at Fort Sumter, South Carolina, in April 1861, Doubleday had the distinction of firing the federal response to Confederate cannonade during the siege that marked the beginning of hostilities in the Civil War.

Doubleday later served in most of the major campaigns in the eastern theater of operations, fighting in the battles of Manassas, Antietam, Fredericksburg, and Gettysburg. At Gettysburg, Doubleday assumed temporary command of General Reynolds' "I Corps" after the commander was killed during the first day of fighting. Under Doubleday's leadership, two Confederate brigades were virtually annihilated and his troops helped repel Pickett's charge on the last, crucial day of the battle.

Despite such valor and notable service, Doubleday is most remembered for something he neither did nor claimed – the founding of baseball. Several years after his death, a commission was created in 1907 to investigate the origins of the national pastime. Headed by Albert Spalding, the commission reported that, "Baseball had its origin in the United States [and that it] was devised by Abner Doubleday at Cooperstown, New York in 1839."

Doubleday's name and the city of Cooperstown, the home of baseball's Hall of Fame, became forever linked to the game despite historical evidence that clearly refuted the Spalding committee's findings. Indeed, Doubleday was not even in Cooperstown during 1839 and in his copious writings, which include thousands of pages of diaries, letters, and speeches, there is not the slightest mention of baseball. Still, the myth remains strong and, to most Americans, Abner Doubleday continues to be the "Father of Baseball."

The burial of such notable figures as Doubleday, Tanner, and MacArthur enhanced Arlington's new identity as a national cemetery. By the end of the 19th century, it had become the most widely known of the national cemeteries. It truly reflected the spirit of Theodore O'Hara's poem whose verses were strategically placed on bronze plaques through the cemetery:

> On fame's eternal camping ground
> Their silent tents are spread
> And glory guards with solemn round
> The bivouac of the dead.

CHAPTER FOUR

Where Valor Proudly Sleeps

—*Theodore O'Hara*

In 1886, John Commerford, a partially disabled Civil War veteran, was appointed superintendent of Arlington National Cemetery. He moved into the Lee mansion, which had been converted into a residence for the cemetery's chief administrator. Commerford was enthusiastically described in an early inspection report as "...intelligent, well-educated, energetic, and capable." The report went on to declare, "...the general condition of the cemetery was good," but also warned that, "Being in the vicinity, there are, in spite of the difficulty in getting there, many visitors, many of them rough characters."

The greatest problem facing Commerford in the late 19th century was cemetery expansion. Arlington's original 200 acres now contained the remains of over 19,000 soldiers and servicemen. With slightly over 300 interments annually, the cemetery would soon be unable to accommodate further burials without a major acquisition of new acreage. The logical area for expansion was to the southwest toward the Freedmen's Village, which continued to operate within the confines of the original Lee estate.

After the government's settlement with Custis Lee in 1883, all doubt concerning the ownership of Arlington had been removed. Legally, the former Lee estate was now an Army reservation and subject to government regulations that technically prohibited civilians from residing on a military post.

On November 12, 1887, Superintendent Commerford directed a letter to the Deputy Quartermaster General of the Army requesting the eviction of African-American residents from the premises claiming that the inhabitants were frequently trespassing on the cemetery grounds and pilfering firewood:

> I would respectfully report that for years past some of the colored people who live on the reservation have been in the habit of entering the cemetery during the late hours of the night for the purpose of getting wood for fuel.
>
> On my arrival here, one year ago, I was informed that several hundred young forest trees, from 2 to 6 inches in diameter were cut down and carried away. The remains of those trees can yet be seen.

Library of Congress

A view of the Arlington House Mansion circa 1900. By the turn of the century, Arlington had acquired additional acreage of land and had become the largest operating national cemetery

It has been the custom of these thieves, to use a cross cut saw to cut down tress. By so doing, very little noise is made, in order to avoid detection. It is said, that very few of these squatters buy any fuel, and depend mostly on what they can pick up within the enclosure. It would be necessary for a man to remain on watch all night, to arrest the guilty parties. It has been suggested, that the most effective way of preventing such thefts, is to cause the removal of these people from the reservation.

The Quartermaster General's office quickly responded:

In Violation of paragraph #138 Army Regulations, amended by General Order #26, Adjutant General's Office, 1883, civilians are residing upon the Military reservation, upon which the Arlington National Cemetery and the Military Post at Fort Myer, Va., are located.

This occupation has continued many years, and since the title of the land passed to the United States by purchase, May 18, 1883, no steps have been taken for the removal of these occupants, mostly colored people.

In consequence of the complaints now made, it would seem to be proper that they should be ordered to vacate their holdings, giving them sufficient time for moving their property to prevent suffering.

I therefore recommend that the Military Authorities at Fort Myer be directed to serve notice upon all Civilians residing on the reservation, and not employed by the Government, that they must remove therefrom, within 90 days after date of notice.

Over the next few years, the Freedmen's Village slowly disappeared. The cemetery acquired 142 acres in 1889 and an additional 56 acres in 1897. By the turn of the century, Arlington held the distinction of being the largest of the nation's 83 operating national cemeteries.

Federal law required Arlington and all national cemeteries to enclose the grounds with a fence. Arlington used this government mandate to construct three impressive entry gates to the cemetery, memorializing four major Civil War generals — Sheridan, Ord, Weitzel, and McClellan.

The cemetery's main entrance was named for General Philip Sheridan who was buried at Arlington in 1888. The Union cavalry commander gained a reputation for ruthlessness while pursuing Confederate troops through the Shenandoah Valley during the brutal campaigns of 1864 confiscating livestock, burning fields, and destroying harvests. The Sheridan Gate consisted of four stately white columns which had been removed from the old War Department building in Washington before its demolition in 1879. Each pillar was individually inscribed with the name of an additional Civil War figure — Scott, Lincoln, Stanton, and Grant. The large iron gates bore the Latin phrase, "It is sweet and glorious to die for the Fatherland."

Entrance to the lower cemetery, the site of the earliest burials at Arlington, was through the Ord-Weitzel gate, named for Major Generals Edward Ord and Godfrey Weitzel, Union officers during the Civil War. Ord had been a major figure in the capture of Jackson, Mississippi, and was present during the siege of Petersburg. Wietzel was one of the Union Army's most experienced engineers and officer-in-charge of the 1865 occupation forces in Richmond. The gate consisted of twin white pillars, also taken from the old War Department building. After a major land acquisition and the resulting expansion of the cemetery eastward in the late 1960s, both gates were rendered useless and were finally torn down.

The only surviving original gate was named for General George McClellan, the "Young Napoleon," who made his headquarters temporarily at Arlington while in command of federal forces. The large, red sandstone edifice became a model for similar gates in national cemeteries located in Chattanooga, Nashville, and Vicksburg. The McClellan gate, although no longer functional, has been retained for its historical significance. Inscribed above the archway are the cemetery's Civil War statistics: "Here rests 15,585 of the 315,555 Citizens who Died in the Defense of our Country from 1861 to 1865." A portion of Theodore O'Hara's poem appears on the structure as well: "Rest on Embalmed and Sainted Dead, Dear as the Blood ye Gave and Glory Guards with Solemn Round the Bivouac of the Dead." Of the various individuals commemorated by the three gates, only Generals Sheridan and Ord are actually interred at Arlington Cemetery.

In 1892, in an effort to make Arlington cemetery representative of all the nation's wars, four Revolutionary War soldiers – Generals Thomas Meason, James House, Paymaster General Caleb Swan, and LTC William Burrows – were reinterred from their original resting place at the Old Presbyterian Cemetery in Georgetown to Section 1. In addition, fourteen unknowns from the War of 1812 were also buried at Arlington in 1905 after their remains were recovered during renovation of the Washington Barracks. These soldiers were apparently killed during the British assault and burning of the city a century earlier.

The most celebrated figure reinterred during the early 20th century was Major Pierre L'Enfant. L'Enfant, a French national, immigrated to the United States in 1777 and served with the Continental Army in the engineering corps during the American Revolution. After the war and the subsequent adoption of the United States Constitution, Congress authorized the construction of a new federal capital. The city was to be located in the South in "…a district of territory not exceeding ten miles square…on the river Potomac for the permanent seat of Government of the United States." It was literally to be a new city constructed out of the wilderness, completely planned and designed to emphasize the infant nation's republican ideals. The capital was to be completed by December 1800.

Pierre L'Enfant was a skilled and talented draftsman and was commissioned to diagram the layout and to create a metropolis, "...magnificent enough to grace a great nation." He proved, however, to be a temperamental and difficult man and was ultimately dismissed from the project. Major alterations to his original drawings were subsequently made and these were implemented in the final development of the federal city. Angry and embittered, L'Enfant continually petitioned Congress for payment for his services and plans but was unsuccessful in recouping adequate payment. He received only $2,394 for all of his labor and died virtually penniless in 1825. He was buried in obscurity on the Digges Farm in Prince George's County, Maryland. Many decades later, Congress belatedly recognized L'Enfant's contributions to the development of the District of Columbia and, in 1909, his remains were exhumed and brought to the United States Capitol to lie in state in the Rotunda, resting upon the famed Lincoln catafalque. On April 28, 1909, after a series of tributes and memorials, his body was brought to Arlington National Cemetery and buried in a prominent location directly in front of the Arlington House mansion on a hill overlooking the beautiful capital city he had once envisioned. His monument, designed by W.W. Bosworth, bears an engraving of one of L'Enfant's early maps of the District of Columbia.

Spanish-American War

War once again came to the United States in 1898 placing additional demands on Arlington. By the end of the 19th century, the Spanish empire in North America had been reduced to Cuba and a few, small Caribbean islands. Local insurgents, dissatisfied with decades of harsh colonial rule, had begun to rebel, prompting a strong and often brutal Spanish reaction.

On January 25, 1898, as the Caribbean region became more destabilized, President William McKinley ordered the battleship U.S.S. *Maine* to Havana, Cuba, ostensibly to protect American citizens and property but simultaneously to demonstrate the power and might of the United States Navy.

On the night of February 15, 1898, while peacefully docked in the harbor, a powerful explosion occurred on the *Maine* and the ship rapidly sank killing 260 members of the crew. The jingoistic, yellow press in the United States demanded immediate military action and increased popular outrage against Spain with such inflammatory slogans as, "Remember the *Maine* and to Hell with Spain." An American investigation into the sinking was ordered by the President to determine culpability in the explosion. After several weeks of inquiry, the commission concluded that the *Maine* had been sunk by a submarine mine and placed blame squarely on the Spanish government although recent scholarship has discredited this finding.

With public opinion demanding retaliation for the sinking, McKinley

The Maine *dead being returned to the United States for burial at Arlington National Cemetery.*

The battleship Maine *entering Havana harbor. Two weeks later the ship exploded, killing 260 members of the crew*

asked Congress for a formal declaration of war against Spain on April 11, 1898. For the next year, the United States fought what was popularly referred to as, "A splendid little war," which was marked by numerous military victories, major territorial acquisition, and a minimal loss of life. Indeed, the United States military sustained only 385 combat-related fatalities during the entire Spanish-American conflict, but an additional 2,000 servicemen died from various tropical diseases and illnesses. Many remains of these soldiers and sailors were returned from foreign battlefields and stations for burial at Arlington Cemetery in accordance with an 1899 presidential proclamation which stated: "…the remains…of the brave officers and men who perished, there has been reserved interment in ground sacred to the soldiers and sailors…at the National Cemetery at Arlington."

The burial of the Spanish-American War soldiers at Arlington represented the first time in American history that servicemen who served abroad in a foreign war were repatriated to the United States for reinterment. The National Society of Colonial Dames in 1902 erected a monument in Section 22 to honor, "…the soldiers and sailors of the United States who gave their lives for their country in the war of 1898-99 with Spain."

The victims of the *Maine* tragedy, the casus belli of the conflict, were initially buried in the Colon Cemetery in Havana, Cuba. The catastrophic nature of their deaths, however, made individual identification difficult; only 63 of the 160 recovered bodies could actually be positively identified. Fighting on the island in 1898 between American and Spanish forces delayed initial plans for the return of the *Maine* crew to the United States for appropriate burial.

In the following year, the Navy exhumed 151 of the sailors from the Cuban cemetery. Funeral arrangements were complicated because virtually all of the remains had commingled, having been initially interred six to a grave. The Navy, therefore, rejected the requests of family members for individual private interments and insisted instead on burying the dead together as a crew on Hall's Knoll at Arlington National Cemetery. The 150 flag-draped coffins were transported back to the United States on board the battleship, *Texas*, the sister ship of the *Maine*, now commanded by the sunken vessel's surviving commanding officer, Admiral Charles Dwight Sigsbee.

On December 27, 1899, the coffins were transported to Arlington on horse drawn wagons to await burial scheduled for the following day. The remains were placed under tents with a detachment of Marines deployed to guard them. At 11 o'clock on the morning of December 28, funeral services began despite an untimely Washington snowfall. President William McKinley led the mourners who included the two major naval heroes of the Spanish-American War, Admirals Sigsbee and Dewey.

Individual wreaths were placed upon each coffin during the services, which were concluded with the playing of "Taps." The ceremonies, however, were marred by the presence of aggressive cameramen, eager to photograph the rows of flag-draped coffins lying in open trenches. The *Washington Evening Star* recounted:

> There were seemingly a score of [photographers], in fact, and during the solemn service they made themselves most obnoxious by snapping pictures from every point of view. While the chaplains were praying the camera men were rushing about, setting their machines here and there. Finally several of them actually got between the chaplains and the graves and there snapped

their kodaks. They seemed to have absolutely no regard for the meaning and solemnity of the occasion. A large sign posted by the cemetery authorities to the effect that no pictures shall be made of funeral services at Arlington was evidently disregarded. Once the photographers were within the grounds to have stopped them in their sacrilegious intrusion would have necessitated an interruption of the ceremonies, and this was not at all desirable.

The *Maine,* itself, remained submerged in Havana harbor for 12 years until the United States Congress appropriated funds in 1910 for its salvage and to recover the remaining bodies of the 66 sailors still entombed on the ship and to provide "...for proper interment of the bodies...in Arlington Cemetery." After Naval recovery efforts successfully retrieved the bodies of the crew, the ship's masts were removed before the *Maine* was towed out to sea and scuttled. Only one of the recovered bodies from the ship could positively be identified and his remains were returned to family members for private interment. The other 65 sailors remained unknown and they were buried at Arlington Cemetery alongside their compatriots.

A memorial to the Maine dead was dedicated on February 15, 1915, the 17th anniversary of the ship's sinking. It is situated adjacent to the graves of the sailors who had served on the vessel. The focal point of the monument is the *Maine*'s mast which is mounted on a simulated battleship gun turret. The names of all 260 casualties of the ship's explosion have been inscribed on the base. The ship's foremast is on the campus of the U.S. Navel Academy in Annapolis, Maryland, overlooking the Chesapeake Bay.

The Confederate Memorial

In 1906, Congress authorized the construction of a Confederate memorial at Arlington Cemetery. Moses Ezekiel, a southern veteran of the Battle of New Market and a renowned artist and sculptor, was commissioned to design and cast the monument. On June 4, 1914, the birthday of Jefferson Davis, the Confederate Memorial was formally dedicated with President Woodrow Wilson delivering the principal address.

The monument's central feature is a bronze female figure representing the south in peace. Facing south in the direction of the former Confederacy, she holds a plow stock symbolically referring to the Biblical passage from the book of Isaiah, "They shall beat their swords into plow shares." The principal inscription pays tribute to all southern soldiers and reads:

Not for fame or reward
Not for place or for rank
Not lured by ambition

Or goaded by necessity
But in simple
Obedience to duty
As they understood it
These men suffered all
Sacrificed all
Dared all – and died.

All 409 Confederate soldiers who remained buried at Arlington were re-interred to Jackson Circle and buried in a circular pattern around the base of the memorial. The southern gravestones, however, are slightly different from their Union counterparts, coming to a slight point at the top. Popular legend maintains that these pointed stones were originally designed to keep Yankees from sitting on the graves of their former foes.

The Confederate Memorial. The monument commemorates the 409 southern soldiers buried at Arlington.

Early Aviation

During the period following the Spanish-American War, the United States Army began efforts to modernize. Experiments by the Wright brothers with a heavier than air flying machine had drawn particular interest from the Army which saw the invention as potentially useful for airborne observation of hostile troops. Thus, the United States Signal Corps challenged potential developers to test their new aircraft before a panel of military observers at Fort Myer, Virginia, immediately adjacent to Arlington National Cemetery. The Signal Corps specifications required that a suitable plane must be capable of carrying a minimum of two passengers at 40 miles per hour for at least 60 minutes of sustained flight. Supremely confident, Orville Wright brought a prototype airplane to Arlington for the trials scheduled for the fall of 1908.

National Archives

Orville Wright demonstrating his new airplane at Fort Myer, Virginia in 1908. Lt. Thomas Selfridge was killed in a subsequent flight when the plane crashed near the cemetery's west gate which is visible in the foreground.

The spectacle of manned flight drew large crowds to the military post, including such notables as Secretary of War and presidential hopeful, William Howard Taft. For the next several days, Wright gave repeated successful demonstrations before the panel of impressed observers. On September 17, 1908, a young Army lieutenant, Thomas Selfridge, volunteered to be a passenger on one of Wright's test flights. Shortly after takeoff, one of the aircraft's propellers split and the plane lost control, plummeting to the ground near the western wall of Arlington Cemetery. Wright was seriously injured in the crash and Selfridge, despite receiving immediate medical attention at the scene, died a few hours later at Walter Reed Medical Hospital from the injuries he sustained. Selfridge was buried with full military honors at Arlington National Cemetery, the first casualty of modern aviation. In his honor, the western gate to the cemetery near the original crash site was renamed the Selfridge Gate.

The Memorial Amphitheater

In 1914, all of the major European powers went to war after the assassination of the Austrian-Hungarian Archduke, Franz Ferdinand. President Woodrow Wilson was determined to avoid American involvement in the distant conflict and urged the nation to remain neutral in thought as well as deeds.

The dedication ceremonies of the Memorial Amphitheater.

On October 13, 1915, ceremonies were conducted at Arlington National Cemetery to mark the beginning of construction of a new Memorial Amphitheater. The building, authorized by Congress in 1913, was designed to accommodate Memorial Day crowds of up to 5,000 people and provide a suitable place for other commemorative services.

The theme for the services was, "Lest We Forget," with the principal address delivered by the Secretary of the Navy, Josephus Daniels. Daniels reminded the assembled crowd of the substantial role Arlington played in United States history: "Perpetual be the national spirit that brings annually on a pilgrimage to this spot the national consciousness and the national conscience. Here is the heart of the Republic." He went on to explain the noble goals of all the nation's wars in which many of Arlington's dead had fought:

> It is a good thing to recognize the character of our wars. Our wars against the Indians were not wars of hatred, but they were to protect life and extend and teach civilization. The revolution was for liberty. The war of 1812 was for liberty on sea as well as on land. The Mexican war was to protect our borders. Our civil war was the chastening of a nation to make it see its destiny when it would not…The Spanish war gave liberty to millions and guaranteed republics for all portions of the American hemisphere. All the wars which we have ever waged were to get liberty for ourselves or to give it to others. Life is not so sweet as liberty.

A 35-star Civil War-era flag was flown at half-staff throughout the opening ceremonies on a flagpole specially erected for the occasion. President Woodrow Wilson laid the cornerstone to the Amphitheater. It contained designs for the structure, an autographed photo of the President, and a copy of the day's program along with various other memorabilia from the period. Once the stone was in place, the Civil War flag was replaced with a new, 48-star banner, symbolizing the recent completion of American continental expansion. President Wilson's participation in the Amphitheater ceremonies established the precedent for presidential visits to the building, a tradition that has been continued by all of his successors during their tenures as chief executive.

The years after 1914 saw an increase in tension between the United States and the European belligerents. The sinking of the *Lusitania* combined with reports of German atrocities in neutral Belgium, enraged the American population. Still, during the 1916 presidential campaign, Wilson adopted the slogan, "He Kept Us out of War." That same year, during Memorial Day services at the Old Amphitheater, Wilson used the occasion to urge all American young men to volunteer for military service and warned Germany that the United States was prepared, "…to become partners in any alliance of nations that would guarantee public right above selfish aggression."

In 1917, after the Germans initiated a policy of unlimited submarine warfare, several American ships were sunk in international waters by patrolling U-boats. The United States Congress adopted a formal declaration of war and, for the first time in the nation's history, American combat troops were sent to liberate Europe. Wilson again used his traditional Arlington Memorial Day address to make a major foreign policy announcement by outlining the noble goals for the United States' entry into the Great War: "We did not set this government up in order that we might have a selfish and separate liberty, for we are now ready to come to [Europe's] assistance and fight out upon the fields of the world the cause of human liberty."

The injection of thousands of fresh American troops into the conflict was sufficient to break the battlefield stalemate and on November 11, 1918, an armistice was declared and the war was brought to a successful conclusion. The United States lost 116,708 soldiers during its short involvement in the war, most of whom were initially buried in France until arrangements could be made for the return of their remains to the United States. During the ensuing years, a constant stream of American war dead were repatriated and consigned to new graves at Arlington.

The onset of military hostilities had delayed the construction of the Memorial Amphitheater and the structure was not completed until 1920. Dedication ceremonies for America's "Temple of Patriotism" were held on May 15, 1920, and were attended by surviving veterans of the Civil War, Spanish-American War, and World War I. President Wilson, still suffering from partial paralysis due to a stroke, was unable to attend the services but the

Library of Congress

Aerial view of the newly completed Memorial Amphitheater, 1920. The Tomb of the Unknown Soldier was not added until the following year. The Confederate Memorial and the Mast of the Maine memorial are visible in the background.

White House did send a wreath to mark the auspicious occasion.

The Memorial Amphitheater commemorates American military leaders and great battles from the Revolution through the Spanish-American War. Over the stage area are words from George Washington: "When we assumed the soldier we did not lay aside the citizen." A portion of Lincoln's Gettysburg Address is also inscribed on the Amphitheater: "We here highly resolve that these dead shall not have died in vain."

The Amphitheater was originally constructed with 48 burial crypts located beneath its colonnade. These were intended to accommodate the remains of "favorite sons" of each of the individual states, but the difficulty in establishing adequate protocol coupled with the subsequent expansion of the nation forced abandonment of the project. Many of the original crypts were demolished during the renovation of the building in 1976 to create office space, modern restroom facilities, and handicapped access. The surviving crypts, popularly referred to as the "catacombs," are now used for storage and for drill practice by members of the Tomb Guard during off-duty days.

The *Shenandoah*

Although the airplane played only a minor role in the outcome of World War I, some visionaries, including General Billy Mitchell, saw the need for an expanded role of aviation in the military. Indeed, Mitchell argued that aircraft could be a potentially decisive weapon.

U.S. Navy Photo

The dirigible Shenandoah *in flight over New Jersey. The airship crashed during a violent thunderstorm in 1925 killing 14 Navy aviators.*

Mitchell's appeal for an air force suffered a serious setback on September 3, 1925, when the Navy's dirigible, *Shenandoah*, crashed in Ohio during a violent thunderstorm. Fourteen Naval aviators died including Mitchell's close friend, Lieutenant Commander Zachary Landsdowne, the commander of the vessel.

Landsdowne and three of his fellow officers were brought to Arlington National Cemetery for funeral services. The four aviation pioneers were interred near the grave of three-time unsuccessful presidential candidate, William Jennings Bryan, just north of Dewey Circle.

Robert Todd Lincoln

On a shaded hill at the cemetery overlooking the Lincoln Memorial is the grave of Robert Todd Lincoln, the eldest son of President Abraham Lincoln. Born in 1843, his three brothers — Eddie, Willie, and Tad — all died before adulthood, leaving only Robert to continue the Lincoln legacy.

During the Civil War, Robert observed his father's greatest crises at a distance while attending Harvard College in Massachusetts. Upon graduation in January 1865, he requested permission to enlist in the Union Army as a private but the President, having already buried two of his children, was reluctant to risk the life of a third in a war that was nearly won. Lincoln wrote to General-in-Chief U.S. Grant, "My son, now in his 22nd year, having graduated at Harvard, wishes to see something of the war before it ends. I do not wish him put in the ranks, nor yet to give him a commission, to which those

P. Bigler

The Lincoln sarcophagus. Robert Todd Lincoln was interred at Arlington in 1926. His wife and son, Abraham Lincoln II, are also buried at the site.

who have already served long, are better entitled, and better qualified to hold." Grant responded by making Robert a captain on his personal staff, a position that allowed the young Lincoln to witness Lee's surrender at Appomatox Courthouse. On April 14, 1865, he recounted the dramatic scene to his father at the White House but fatefully declined an invitation at the same time to attend an evening performance of Laura Keene in "Our American Cousin" at Ford's Theater.

At the theater later that evening, President Lincoln was shot and mortally wounded by John Wilkes Booth. Informed of the shooting while staying at the White House, Robert hurried to the President's deathbed at the Peterson boarding house. There, he tried in vain to comfort his grieving and hysterical mother, Mary Todd, while the President slowly succumbed to his bullet wound.

Mary Todd Lincoln never recovered from her husband's assassination and wore mourning garb for the remainder of her life. Having suffered through the murder of her husband, the loss of two children from disease, and the deaths of three brothers in combat during the Civil War (all ironically fighting for the Confederacy), the death of her youngest son, Tad, in 1871 finally caused her to go insane. Robert Lincoln, the sole heir, was forced to sign the commitment papers confining his mother to a sanitarium. Discharged five years later, Mary Todd vehemently denounced Robert and his wife, Mary Harlan, and claimed preposterously that they coveted her inheritance.

In 1881, President James Garfield appointed Robert Todd Lincoln to his cabinet as Secretary of War. On July 2, Lincoln escorted the President to the Baltimore and Potomac Railroad Station (the current site of the National Gallery of Art) where the President was to embark on a vacation to the New Jersey shore. Instead, Robert watched in horror as a frustrated and mentally deranged office seeker, Charles Guiteau, shot Garfield. The President lingered on for several weeks before finally succumbing to his wounds, thereby becoming the second American chief executive to fall victim to an assassin. Two decades later, on September 6, 1901, Lincoln was attending the Pan-American Exposition in Buffalo, New York, and was present when President William McKinley was assassinated, thereby becoming the only person to be present at three presidential assassinations.

Robert Lincoln had a distinguished political career which included an appointment as the United States Minister to Great Britain under the Benjamin Harrison administration. Lincoln's wife, Mary Harlan, and their son, Abraham "Jack" Lincoln II, accompanied him to his diplomatic post in London. Jack was soon sent to school in Versailles, France, to study the language in preparation for his college entrance exams at Harvard. While there, the boy had a carbuncle or abscess surgically removed from under his left arm. Almost immediately, a serious bacterial infection set in, apparently caused by the use of unsterile instruments during the surgery. Robert Lincoln had his son returned to London to recuperate but Jack died on March 5, 1890, at the age of sixteen. His body was returned to Springfield, Illinois, where it was temporarily interred near his grandfather in the Lincoln mausoleum.

Robert Todd Lincoln went on to become a successful businessman and ultimately a millionaire. Upon his death in 1926, he was buried at Arlington National Cemetery in a plot that commanded a spectacular view of the newly constructed Lincoln Memorial. Mary Harlan, his wife of 58 years, was buried alongside him upon her death a decade later.

The remains of their son, Jack Lincoln, were reinterred to Arlington on May 27, 1930, but existing cemetery regulations allowed for the acknowledgement of a dependent's burial only in, "...the records of the cemetery but the name shall not appear on any monument... [and may be indicated] only with a footstone, sunk flush with the ground." Thus, Jack's only memorial was a small, partially obscured footstone bearing the initials "ALII" placed at the Lincoln gravesite. In December 1983, well after cemetery regulations had been liberalized, Robert Todd Lincoln Beckwith, the only surviving grandson of Robert Lincoln, finally had the name of Abraham Lincoln II inscribed on the gravesite's large marble sarcophagus. Beckwith died without a descendent on December 24, 1985, and the direct Lincoln line ended with his demise.

William Howard Taft

From 1921 through 1948 there was only one state funeral conducted by the United States, that for former President and Chief Justice, William Howard Taft in 1930. Taft graduated from Yale University and gained a national reputation during his astute governorship of the occupied Philippine Islands after the Spanish-American War. He later served as Secretary of War under President Theodore Roosevelt and succeeded him as chief executive in 1909.

In the 1912 presidential contest, Taft was nominated for re-election by the Republican Party. The Democrats, in turn, nominated the popular governor of New Jersey, Woodrow Wilson. Former President, Theodore Roosevelt, hoping to reclaim the presidency after a four year hiatus, mounted a powerful third party challenge, creating the Progressive or Bull Moose Party. With the Republican vote hopelessly split between Taft and Roosevelt, Wilson narrowly won the election and Taft involuntarily retired, later stating, "I do not care for politics. Not that I have no interest in such matters, but because I am not fitted for the mustings and controversy."

After World War I and the return of the Republicans to office in 1921, President Warren G. Harding appointed Taft as Chief Justice of the United States Supreme Court, thereby becoming the only man in history to hold the highest positions in both the executive and judicial branches. Taft excelled in the Supreme Court, delivering over 250 opinions but refused to write any dissenting positions since he preferred not to disagree publicly with his distinguished colleagues.

In February 1930, at the age of 72, Taft retired from the bench because of a persistent heart problem exacerbated by his ample, 300-pound girth. A month later, on March 8, the former President suffered a fatal stroke at his home in Washington, D.C.

On March 10, a 48-gun salute (one for each state) to the Union was fired in his honor, the traditional acknowledgement of the death of a chief executive. Funeral plans were formalized by his family who, in accordance with Taft's wishes, selected a grave in what was then a secluded and quiet location at Arlington National Cemetery.

President Herbert Hoover declared an official 30-day mourning period and Taft's body was brought to the Capitol to lie in state in the Rotunda. Funeral services were held on March 11 at the All Soul's Unitarian Church on 16th Street. The body was then escorted to Arlington for appropriate services.

Taft became the first American President to be interred at Arlington National Cemetery. Each year on his birthday, September 15, the incumbent president sends a wreath to the grave which is placed with full military honors. Similar services are held at all presidential gravesites on the deceased executive's respective birthday.

CHAPTER FIVE

Under My Eternal Vigilance

—Sentinels's Creed

World War I saw the development of new and terrible technologies from the machine gun to poison gases, all of which contributed to unprecedented human destruction. During the four years of sustained combat between 1914 and 1918, the warring powers suffered over eight million battlefield casualties. The civilian populations were forced to endure famines and epidemics while being subjected to constant shortages of food and medicine.

After the war, the British and French governments attempted to bring some meaning to the slaughter by interring an unknown soldier in a place of supreme honor to symbolically represent and pay tribute to all of those who had perished. In 1920, the remains of an unidentified English soldier were disinterred and returned from France in a simple pine coffin draped with the British Union Jack. The body was taken to Westminster Abbey for funeral services, which were attended by King George V and thousands of widows and Gold Star mothers. During the extensive ceremonies, the King presented the British Unknown with a saber inscribed: "A British Warrior who fell in the Great War 1914/1918." The casket was finally committed to a specially prepared crypt in the abbey that had been filled earlier with soil taken from the battlefields of France where the British soldier had undoubtedly died.

Simultaneously, the French were entombing an Unknown Soldier from their nation at the base of the *Arc de Triomphe* in ceremonies planned to coincide with the British services. The *London Times* reported:

> At the very hour when the Unknown British Warrior to 'the noise of an Empire's lamination' – and proud rejoicing – was being borne to his last home at Westminster, an Unknown French Warrior, his faithful companion in arms was being carried to the *Arc de Triomphe*, there to remain throughout the ages as a symbol of that suffering and glory of which in his life and in his death he achieved his just share.

With the burials of the French and British Unknown Soldiers, other

European nations that had participated in the Great War likewise undertook plans to honor anonymous soldiers from their own countries. The Italian ceremonies, conducted in Rome on November 4, 1921, were marred by factionalism and political dissent, an ominous harbinger of future European hostilities. The *London Times* reported:

> Communists were in the crowds, wearing their badges with hammer and scythe; Fascisti, in black shirts embroidered with skull and cross-bones; mothers proudly displaying the medals won by their dead sons; little school children dressed in white, clustering around bespectacled priests; maimed soldiers who are carried on stretchers; blinded soldiers who wanted to hear though they cannot see the ceremony.

The United States did not undertake any substantive plans for the burial of an American Unknown Soldier until after the conclusion of the 1920 presidential contest. Shortly thereafter, legislation sponsored by Congressman Hamilton Fish of New York was adopted, authorizing the return of an Unknown American Soldier from Europe and for burial at Arlington National Cemetery on the plaza of the newly completed Memorial Amphitheater.

American combat involvement in World War I had been brief, lasting just a single year. During that time, 99 percent of all American casualties were positively identified and buried in marked graves. Still, by 1921, there were 1,237 soldiers from the American Expeditionary Forces (AEF) whose remains were classified as unidentifiable. Four of these bodies were exhumed from different cemeteries in France, each denoting a theater of operations where American forces had been engaged. After it was verified that these anonymous soldiers had indeed fought with the AEF and that their deaths were combat related, they were officially declared candidates for the nation's Unknown Soldier.

The four bodies of the American soldiers were placed in identical caskets and brought to Charlons-sur-Marne for a formal selection ceremony on October 24, 1921. Sergeant Edward F. Younger, Headquarters Co., 2d Battalion, 50th Infantry, US Army, a highly decorated combat infantryman, was given the honor of choosing the American Unknown. Younger made his selection by placing a single white rose on one of the coffins. Later he commented: "I went into the room and walked past the caskets. I walked around them three times. Suddenly I stopped. It was as though something had pulled me. A voice seemed to say: 'This is a pal of yours.' "

The remains of the designated Unknown Soldier from World War I were then taken to the port city of Le Harve for transport back to the United States. The cruiser U.S.S. *Olympia*, the famous flagship of Admiral George Dewey, was commissioned to make the Atlantic crossing. The remaining unselected candidates were immediately taken to the Romagne Cemetery and reburied to ensure the perpetual anonymity of the American Unknown.

Interment services at Arlington National Cemetery were officially scheduled for Armistice Day, November 11, 1921. President Warren G. Harding, honoring a Congressional Resolution, proclaimed the day a national holiday: Whereas Armistice Day, November 11, 1921, has been designated as the appropriate time for the ceremonies incident to the burial of the unknown and unidentified soldier in the Arlington National Cemetery...

> Whereas this unknown soldier represents the manhood of America who gave their lives to defend its integrity, honor and tranquility against any enemy, and
>
> Whereas the nations of the earth are on that date joining with the United States in paying respect and homage to this unknown soldier, therefore be it,
>
> Resolved...[to declare] November 11, 1921, a holiday.

The *Olympia* arrived at the Washington, D.C. Navy Yard on November 9, and the casket of the Unknown was conveyed to the Rotunda to lie in state upon the Lincoln catafalque. A joint service honor guard was deployed around the coffin to maintain a continual vigil throughout the period of pub-

The caisson bearing the remains of the World War I Unknown Soldier at the Capitol. General John J. Pershing served as an honorary pallbearer.

lic viewing. During the next two days, while the Unknown Soldier laid in state at the Capitol, over 90,000 people quietly filed by the bier to pay their respects.

On the morning of November 11, the casket was placed upon a horse-drawn caisson for the final journey to the cemetery. The accompanying funeral procession on foot was led by President Warren G. Harding and Chief Justice of the Supreme Court William Howard Taft. Former president Woodrow Wilson, still suffering the debilitating effects of a stroke, participated but was forced to ride in an open carriage.

Huge crowds amassed along the funeral route watched solemnly as the coffin passed slowly by. However, at the sight of former President Wilson, spontaneous cheers and applause disrupted the silence. The *New York Times* observed "It was apparent that the sight of Wilson, his once strong body broken by ill-health, his limbs too frail to permit his marching with the other great men who followed the Unknown caisson on foot, was a grim reminder that he had been an outstanding figure in the world conflict which today's ceremonial typified."

When the funeral procession reached the White House, Wilson, physically unable to attend the burial rites at Arlington, was forced to leave the funeral procession. President Harding and members of the official party also decided at this point to drive the remaining distance to the cemetery.

The caisson and the remnants of the procession continued its solemn pace through Georgetown and crossed over the Potomac into Virginia by way of the Aqueduct Bridge (the Memorial Bridge had not yet been built). Harding and the other dignitaries attempted to cross the river via the Highway Bridge located south of the city but an accident on the span obstructed traffic and caused massive delays. Many of the dignitaries hopelessly abandoned their vehicles and decided to walk the substantial distance to Arlington, thereby further exacerbating the traffic problems. Others tried to commandeer small boats docked along the river in a desperate effort to reach the west bank before the funeral services began. Even the presidential motorcade was stalled by the colossal traffic jam. The *Washington Evening Star* reported, "...the president's limousine had to mount the earth and circle through the grass plots of Potomac Park." Despite even these Herculean efforts, President Harding and his entourage still arrived late at Arlington.

When the horse-drawn caisson reached the Memorial Amphitheater, the flag-draped coffin was carried to the apse and placed upon a catafalque located on the stage. Over 5,000 people had crowded into the amphitheater for the funeral service while an additional 100,000 stood along the ridges of Arlington Heights, listening to the funeral ceremony over large loud speakers specially erected for the occasion by the Army.

After a two-minute period of silent tribute and a brief musical interlude, President Harding delivered the eulogy to the Unknown Soldier:

Standing today on hallowed ground, conscious that all America
has halted to share in the tribute of the heart and mind and soul
to this fellow-American…it is fitting to say that his sacrifice, and
that of the millions of dead, shall not be in vain. There must be,
there shall be, the commanding voice of a conscious civilization
against armed warfare.

As we return this poor clay to its mother soil, garlanded by love
and covered with the decorations that only nations can bestow,
I can sense the prayers of our people, of all peoples, that this
Armistice Day shall mark the beginning of a new and lasting era,
of peace on earth, good-will among men.

At the conclusion of his remarks, President Harding awarded the
American Unknown Soldier with the nation's two highest decorations for
valor, the Congressional Medal of Honor and the Distinguished Service
Cross. The casket was then conveyed to the plaza area for the final committal services. Prayers were rendered by members of the clergy as the body was
slowly lowered into the crypt layered with French soil.

Chief Plenty Coup, a Crow Indian representing all native Americans,
stepped forward and spontaneously placed his war bonnet and coup sticks on

*The committal services of the World War I Unknown at Arlington Cemetery. Chief Plenty
Coup later removed his war bonnet and placed it on the Tomb in honor of America's
"Unknown Warrior."*

The Tomb was placed under a daylight military guard in 1926. A decade later, the 24-hour vigil was established. The 50-ton marble cap stone was not added until 1932.

the sarcophagus in tribute to the Unknown Soldier. The newspapers reported "When the aged Indian, with finely chiseled profile, removed his own feathered war bonnet and placed it tenderly on the marble edge of the sarcophagus and then lifted his arms in supplication toward Heaven, it constituted one of the outstanding features of the whole ceremony."

The Tomb of the Unknown Soldier quickly became the nation's most revered shrine to American servicemen. During its early years, the Tomb was protected only by a civilian watchman. In 1926, a formal military guard was established but was maintained only during the daylight hours when the cemetery was open to the public.

The original Tomb consisted only of a modest pedestal base. In 1926, architect Lorimer Rich won the commission to design a more elaborate and suitable monument. A 50-ton piece of Colorado marble was positioned on the original base and was then carefully sculpted to its present shape by Thomas Hudson Jones. The project was finally completed and opened to the public on April 9, 1932. On the front (east side) of the shrine are three figures representing Peace, Victory, and Valor. The phrase, "Here Rests in Honored Glory An American Soldier Known but to God" has been inscribed on the façade facing the Amphitheater. Although the author of these words remains unidentified, the same phrase is etched on the gravestones of all unknown soldiers buried in American cemeteries located throughout the world.

A small crack in the original marble of the Tomb was first discovered in the late 1930s. Over the years, water seeped into the crevice and combined with seasonal freezing and thawing, slowly deepened the fissure. All repair efforts to patch the crack have failed and in 1989, a report recommended that the marble either be replaced or totally enclosed in a weather-proof structure to prevent further damage.

In 2003, efforts were begun to find a piece of marble suitable for an exact replica of Lorimer Rich's original design. The Yule Quarry Company reopened its Colorado mine specifically for this purpose but was unable to excavate a piece of marble large enough to meet Arlington's needs. Currently, alternative sources are being explored in Vermont and it is hoped that a new stone can be located in the immediate future.

The Memorial Gateway

Throughout the cemetery's first 75 years of existence, access from Washington was limited to only two bridges across the Potomac River. A third span, the Memorial Bridge, was constructed between 1926 and 1932. The neo-classical structure was designed to be a "memorial to American patriotism" and, according to the *Washington Evening Star* it was to "... [unite] the city of the dead with the political center of the nation."

The Lincoln Memorial commanded the eastern axis of the Memorial Bridge while the new Memorial Gateway to Arlington Cemetery provided its western terminus. The Memorial Gateway added two new entryways into the cemetery, the Schley and Roosevelt gates, named for Admiral Winfield Scott Schley, commander of naval forces during the battle of Santiago, and President Theodore Roosevelt.

The Memorial Bridge and its mall approaches to Arlington National Cemetery symbolically united the north and south, forever dispelling the sectional differences that had earlier erupted into civil war. Arlington had become a place of pilgrimage for the nation and it's national shrine. Judge Ivory Kimbell, a commander of the Grand Army of the Republic eloquently asserted, "Arlington is not for the burial of the soldiers and sailors of this generation alone. As long as the nation has armies and navies it will be used to bury its soldiers and sailor heroes."

World War II and Korea

After the outbreak of World War II, public sentiment favored interring another unknown soldier at the Tomb to honor servicemen from that conflict. Preliminary planning for such a burial was undertaken shortly after the Japanese surrender with an interment tentatively scheduled for 1951. The World War II Unknown would be buried in an identical tomb constructed on the mall area just below the grave of his World War I compatriot.

In 1950, after the massive invasion of South Korea by Communist forces, all ceremonial planning ceased. Three years of combat followed and a cease-

National Archives

The World War II and Korean Unknown Servicemen lying in state at the Capitol Rotunda, 1958.

fire was not negotiated until 1953. With a return to peace, Congress decided to honor veterans of both World War II and Korea by authorizing the burial of two Unknown Servicemen at Arlington, one from each of the nation's most recent wars.

By the end of World War II, 87,411 Americans remained missing. Many had been lost at sea or killed in catastrophic air accidents. In Korea, 9,037 were still listed as missing in action. These numbers included the 8,526 World War II and the 848 Korean War remains, which had been recovered but were physically unidentifiable and buried without any knowledge of the servicemen's true identities. From these remains, the two new American Unknown Soldiers were to be selected.

For logistical reasons, the burials of the World War II and Korean Unknowns were to be conducted simultaneously on Memorial Day, May 30, 1958. It was then decided to bury the soldiers in two identical crypts flanking the grave of the World War I Unknown and to mark the burials with simple, flat, white memorial stones.

Greatly complicating the selection process of the World War II Unknown was the fact that the war had been fought in two geographically distant theaters. Since it was desirable that the representative Unknown should not be identifiable as to region, two World War II candidates – one from the Pacific Theater and one from the Europe/North Africa Theater – would be chosen. These bodies, in turn, would be brought together in separate but indistinguishable caskets with one finally designated as the Unknown Serviceman from World War II.

On May 12, 1958, at the Epinal American Military Cemetery and Memorial in France, 13 unidentified American remains from Europe and North Africa were brought together for the final selection process. Major General Edward O'Neill, U.S. Army, placed a wreath before one of the coffins, thereby designating the remains as a candidate for America's World War II Unknown Serviceman. Four days later at Hickam Air Force Base, Hawaii, six Pacific casualties were brought together. Colonel Glenn Eagleston, U.S. Air Force, similarly placed a lei on one of the coffins, thereby selecting the Pacific candidate. The Korean Unknown was selected by Master Sergeant Ned Lyle, U.S. Army, in separate ceremonies at the Punchbowl

National Archives

President Dwight D. Eisenhower and Vice President Richard M. Nixon at the double interment of the World War II and Korean Unknowns.

National Cemetery on the island of Oahu on May 15, 1958.

The three bodies were then transported to a predetermined location off Cape Henry, Virginia. There, the remains were brought on board the U.S.S. *Canberra* where the bodies were transferred to new, identical bronze caskets. The Korean Unknown Serviceman was brought to the deck of the ship and placed between the two World War II candidates who were now indistinguishable as to region. First Class William R. Charette, the Navy's only active duty Medal of Honor recipient, placed a floral wreath before one of the caskets, thereby completing the World War II designation process.

During the ceremonies on the *Canberra*, Rear Admiral Levis S. Parks paid tribute to the three Unknown Servicemen: "These men did not fail us when the chips were down and we must not fail them in the days and years ahead when communist forces will press ever harder to drive the free world into slavery. It is not necessary that we know their names. It is enough that they were our comrades and shipmates." At the conclusion of his remarks, the remains of the unselected World War II candidate were buried at sea.

The Korean and World War II Unknown Servicemen were transferred to the U.S.S. *Blandy* for the final journey back to Washington, D.C. The ship docked at the Washington Navy Yard on May 27, 1958. The Unknowns were guarded overnight by two sailors on the fantail of the ship. The following morning, the caskets were taken to the Capitol Rotunda to lie in state with Vice President Richard M. Nixon presiding over the formal Congressional ceremonies.

On Memorial Day, May 30, the caskets were placed on two caissons for the journey to Arlington Cemetery. Along the funeral route, over 100,000 people watched the procession. As the caissons reached the Memorial Bridge, 20 jets flew overhead, minus one plane in the traditional missing man formation.

The joint funeral services were held at the Memorial Amphitheater and were attended by 216 surviving Medal of Honor recipients. Due to the unseasonably hot temperature, over 400 spectators collapsed during the weather-abbreviated ceremonies.

President Eisenhower did not deliver a formal address but did award the Medal of Honor to each of the Unknown Servicemen stating, "On behalf of a grateful people I now present Medals of Honor to these two Unknowns who gave their lives for the United States of America."

The bodies were carried to the plaza by joint service casket teams where President Eisenhower and Vice President Nixon positioned themselves before the respective coffins of the World War II and Korean Unknowns. The bodies were committed later that evening with the white memorial stones sealing the two crypts. They were later engraved with the dates of American involvement in the two wars: 1941-1945 (World War II) and 1950-1953 (Korea).

Vietnam

As the nation was completing the burials of the two Unknowns,

American involvement in the war in Southeast Asia was gradually escalating. Motivated by the fear of communism spreading throughout the region and jeopardizing American interest in the Far East, the United States began to send massive amounts of military aid and supplies to the besieged non-com-

The funeral procession for the Unknown Serviceman from the Vietnam Conflict

munist government of South Vietnam. Likewise, as the war intensified, American military advisors were committed to the region to train the South Vietnamese (A.R.V.N.) military forces. By the end of the Kennedy administration in 1963, over 16,000 American troops were in Vietnam, ostensibly as noncombatants.

After the Gulf of Tonkin incident in August 1964, President Lyndon B. Johnson dispatched the first American combat troops to Vietnam the following March. Ultimately, American troop strength peaked at 500,000 men and by 1968, American military forces were sustaining over 500 combat-related fatalities weekly. Domestically, the war became increasingly unpopular and opposition to American involvement swelled, primarily on the nation's college campuses. President Johnson, rather than risk political defeat at the polls, withdrew from the contentious 1968 presidential contest, ultimately conceding the presidency to the Republican candidate, Richard Nixon.

The Nixon administration pledged to bring about a swift and honorable end to the war and announced the policy of "Vietnamization" in 1969. The policy called for the United States military to turn over responsibility for the war gradually to the Army of the Republic of South Vietnam while allowing the United States to slowly disengage. By 1973, all American combat troops had been effectively withdrawn from South Vietnam after a peace agreement had been signed in Paris. Two years later, however, the nation collapsed after a major North Vietnamese military offensive resulted in the re-unification of Vietnam under a communist government.

As American involvement in Southeast Asia lessened, Congress authorized the entombment of an American Unknown Serviceman from the Vietnam conflict. The Ford administration soon ordered the construction of a new crypt on the plaza of the Memorial Amphitheater between the graves of the World War II and Korean Unknowns to accommodate the remains. Plans for the burial, however, were suspended. Rapid helicopter evacuation and sophisticated forensic techniques had resulted in the identification of all American casualties returned from Vietnam. Indeed, the pathologists at the United States Army Central Identification Laboratory in Hawaii had proved to be remarkably skilled in identifying bodies through the use of dental records, superimposing photographs over skeletal remains, and blood typing.

It was not until a decade after the end of the war that one body was certified unidentifiable and only after a major revision to the rigorous standards historically required for certification of an unknown. On April 17, 1984, Secretary of Defense Caspar Weinberger announced that this soldier would be designated the Unknown Serviceman from the Vietnam Conflict and would be entombed at Arlington National Cemetery on Memorial Day.

For the first time since the custom of designating an Unknown Serviceman was established, no selection ceremony was possible. Instead, on May 17, 1984, at Pearl Harbor, Hawaii, Sergeant Major Allan Kellogg, U.S. Marine Corps, a Medal of Honor recipient, placed a wreath before the single coffin officially recognizing the remains as the Unknown Serviceman form the Vietnam Conflict. The body was then placed on board a naval vessel and returned to the mainland.

The Vietnam Unknown Serviceman arrived in Washington, D.C. on May 25. The remains were conveyed to the Capitol to lie in state over the Memorial Day weekend. During the three-day period, over 250,000 Americans visited the Rotunda to pay their respects to the Unknown. On Memorial Day, May 28, the coffin was placed on a caisson and transported to Arlington Cemetery, pausing briefly en route before the new Vietnam Memorial erected in tribute to the 58,000 Americans who had died during that war. As the procession crossed the Memorial Bridge, an unofficial delegation of Vietnam era veterans, many dressed in military fatigues and wearing their unit insignia and medals, joined their comrade-in-arms following his casket to the entrance to the cemetery.

At the Memorial Amphitheater, President Ronald Reagan delivered an eloquent eulogy to the Unknown Serviceman:

> The unknown soldier who has returned to us today and who we
> lay to rest is symbolic of all our missing sons...About him, we

U.S. Army Photo

A decade after the Vietnam Conflict had concluded, an Unknown from that war was interred at Arlington Cemetery. President Ronald Reagan delivered the eulogy during the funeral services in the Memorial Amphitheater. The remains were later identified as those of Captain Michael Blassie, U.S.A.F.

may well wonder as others have: As a child, did he play on some street in a great American city? Did he work beside his father on a farm in America's heartland? Did he marry? Did he have children? Did he look expectantly to return to a bride? We will never know the answers to those questions about his life. We do know, though, why he died. He saw the horrors of war but bravely faced them, certain his own cause and country's cause was a noble one, that he was fighting for human dignity, for free men everywhere. Today, we pause, to embrace him and all who served us so well in a war whose end offered no parades, no flags, and so little thanks…A grateful nation opens her heart today in gratitude for their sacrifice, for their courage and their noble service. Let us, if we must, debate the lessons learned at some other time. Today we simply say with pride: Thank you, dear son, and may God cradle you in His loving arms.

The body of the Vietnam Unknown Serviceman was buried in the center crypt, immediately in front of the tomb of the World War I Unknown. The white crypt cover was inscribed with the dates, 1958-1975, the period of American involvement in Vietnam.

Identification

In 1977, Charles R. Ford, the Assistant Secretary of the Army (Civil Works), wrote an official memorandum concerning Congressional demands for the interment of a Vietnam Unknown: "I believe the goals of the criteria [for selecting the Unknown] should be to reasonably insure that the remains selected are those of a member of the Armed Forces of the United States, and will not be identified at some future date…with current technology, we may be successful in identifying all recovered remains, at least to a degree which would preclude their candidacy for the Unknown." In an attached information paper, it was further asserted that: "Of the six unidentified [remains at the US Army Central Identification Laboratory], four have been name associated. That is, circumstances surrounding the recovery of the remains provide good indication as to identity, but a comparison of the remains with health and dental records has not established proof beyond any reasonable doubt. The remaining two cannot be confirmed to be American personnel."

In 1998, the family of United States Air Force Captain, Michael Blassie, requested that the military reopen its investigation concerning the identity of the Vietnam Unknown. Strong circumstantial evidence along with new advances in medical technology indicated that the remains interred at Arlington could be those of any one of nine M.I.A.'s (Missing in Action) with the strongest evidence pointing toward either Capt. Blassie or U.S. Army helicopter pilot, Capt. Rodney Strobridge. Both men had been shot down on

May 11, 1972, in a heavily jungled region near An Loc where the Vietnam Unknown's remains were discovered some six months later by an A.R.V.N. patrol. The Pentagon, fully committed to a complete accounting of all servicemen still missing from the war in Southeast Asia, agreed to the disinterment in order to perform DNA testing on the recovered remains.

A plywood construction fence was erected around the crypt area and the Tomb of the Unknown Soldier. Camouflage netting was positioned over the area to protect the dignity of the shrine and to prevent unwanted aerial photography. On the night of May 13/14, the marble crypt cover was carefully removed under the watchful eye of the Tomb Sentinels who maintained their vigil during the entire procedure. Before dawn the next morning, the casket had been removed and the plaza had been completely restored to its original appearance in preparation for a scheduled 10 AM ceremony. Evidence tape was placed around the Unknown's coffin, which was draped with a new American flag and protected by a plastic rain cover. Secretary of Defense William Cohen presided at the service, acknowledging, "We disturb this hallowed ground with profound reluctance. And we take this step only because of our abiding commitment to account for every warrior who fought and died to preserve the freedoms that we cherish." Prayers were rendered and, at the conclusion of the brief ceremonies, the flag-draped casket was carried by a joint service honor guard to an awaiting hearse, saluted by the Commanding General of the Military District of Washington and a Vietnam Medal of Honor recipient, Major General Robert Foley. From Arlington, the Unknown was transported to the Armed Forces Institute of Pathology at Walter Reed where MtDNA testing was to be performed. A few weeks later, the test results conclusively established that the remains were, in fact, those of Captain Blassie. They were then returned to his family for private burial at the Jefferson Barracks National Cemetery in St. Louis, Missouri, on July 11, 1998. Inscribed on the back of Capt. Blassie's standard white gravestone is a listing of his medals along with the acknowledgement that he was America's Vietnam Unknown from May 28, 1984, through May 14, 1998.

After the identification of the remains, Secretary Cohen acknowledged, "…it would seem to me that given the state of art today, it's unlikely that we'll have future unknowns." The center crypt on the plaza at Arlington in now empty but the white memorial stone still remains and is inscribed: "Honoring and Keeping Faith with America's Missing Servicemen, 1958 – 1975," a silent reminder of all of the nation's veterans who served during the Vietnam War.

The Tomb Guard

The three Unknown Servicemen are under a 24-hour honor guard, which was established in 1937. The 3d United States Infantry, "The Old Guard," assumed the duty of protecting the Tomb in 1948. There are three reliefs of sentinels assigned to the Tomb. The soldiers are generally recruited from Fort

J. Dreo

The Changing of the Guard ceremony at the Tomb of the Unknown Soldier.

Myer, Virginia, and must possess both an outstanding military record and an intense desire to become a member of the elite Tomb Guard. Likewise, all must meet the minimum five-foot ten-inch height requirement.

Prospective sentinels first interview with the Sergeant of the Guard and the individual Relief Commander. If deemed acceptable, the soldier is assigned for a two-week probationary period or temporary duty (TDY) where he is introduced to the numerous required duties. Once assigned to Company E (the Tomb Guard), the "New Man" must continue his intense and rigorous training and is expected to work continually to perfect his uniform, to assist the other sentinels in preparing for their "walks," and to learn the history of Arlington Cemetery.

For the next several weeks, the "New Man" is trained by members of his relief in the "catacombs" located under the colonnade area of the Amphitheater. Initially, the soldier is permitted only low visibility walks, a two-hour shift after the cemetery is closed to public visitation and at a time when the Tomb is a restricted military area. Once deemed proficient, he is finally allowed to enter the relief's rotation and is permitted to guard the Tomb on a regularly scheduled basis throughout the day and night.

After nine months of duty, the "New Man" is given a battery of tests. His uniform and walk are carefully scrutinized by the other relief commanders and he is evaluated on his cemetery and military knowledge. Once deemed proficient, the soldier is awarded the Tomb Guard Badge, a silver award which consists of an engraving of the Tomb, an inverted craven wreath, and the words "Honor Guard." The badge is prominently displayed on the right breast pocket of the soldier's uniform. After 12 months of honorable service at the Tomb, the "Badge Holder" is given permanent orders for the decoration and may then wear the Tomb Guard Badge for the duration of his military career, regardless of subsequent rank or branch of the service. Since its inception in 1958, less than 600 sentinels have successfully received permanent orders for the Tomb Guard Badge including Sgt. Heather Johnsen, the first female sentinel, who earned her badge in 1996.

The soldiers at the Tomb are authorized three different uniforms – a blouse, an overcoat, and a raincoat. All are maintained by the individual soldier who must remove and polish all brass and insignia daily to the rigorous standards demanded by the relief commanders. The blouse is made of wool and is worn year-round despite the legendary heat of Washington summers; it is the only fabric that will adequately hold a crease in hot weather. The overcoat is worn only when temperatures are below 45 degrees and the raincoat during periods of inclement weather.

The uniforms, despite public perception, are not tailored; to give the uniform a smooth appearance, all excess material is carefully tucked into the mandatory 29-inch waist belt by assisting sentinels prior to the Guard Change. All the uniforms are dress Army blues reminiscent of the Continental regalia worn by the army during the American Revolution and the Union blue worn by federal troops during the Civil War.

Each soldier is issued a pair of sunglasses for use while guarding the Tomb. Although not considered a traditional part of the regulation military uniform, the sentinels are given a dispensation to wear the glasses since the bright, white marble can induce sunblindness and hinder their mission. The shoes worn by the sentinels are standard Army issue but additional layers of soles have been added to protect the soldiers' feet from heat and cold.

The black mat on the plaza in front of the crypt area is 63 feet long and is replaced each Memorial Day. The sentinel on duty takes 21 steps across the mat, turns, and faces the Tomb for 21 seconds, representative of the highest military tribute—the 21-gun salute.

The Tomb Guard carries an M-14 rifle which is currently issued only to the members of the 3d Infantry and to selected sharpshooter regiments. The weapon weighs 9.5 pounds and is equipped with a chrome, ceremonial bayonet and a black mourning strap. The rifle is always maintained in a position between the visitors and the Tomb, indicating the soldiers' primary mission of protecting the shrine from intruders.

Each relief is on a three-day duty rotation, 24 hours on and 48 hours off. During the off hours, however, the soldiers are expected to practice continually, to prepare their uniforms, and to enhance their knowledge of the cemetery, all the while maintaining standard military skill and combat readiness. During the daylight hours, the Change of the Guard ceremony occurs on the hour in the winter months and on a 30-minute schedule during the summer. At night, the sentinel is on duty for a two-hour shift and is permitted to wear his regular army greens. The guard can sling arms and conducts a perimeter walk around the plaza area but must make a traditional pass along the mat at regular intervals.

The origin of the ceremonial change is obscure. Inspections tended to vary with the personalities of the individual sergeants but are now a standardized procedure with only minor variations permitted. The inspection is genuine. If a sentinel is deemed deficient, he will be ordered by the sergeant back to the quarters to make any necessary uniform corrections. The rifle is also checked for cleanliness by the sergeant who is careful to soak his white cotton gloves with water prior to the inspection to ensure an adequate grip.

Duty at the Tomb is voluntary and sentinels may leave to return to the company at any time. Most, however, chose to remain between 12 and 18 months and view their tour at Arlington as the highlight of their military careers. Indeed, the sentinels believe their duty is a small tribute compared to the ultimate sacrifice offered by the Unknowns who lost their lives to protect the ideals of the nation. Their belief is reflected in the Sentinel's Creed which is memorized by all of the guards and which encapsulates their feelings:

> My dedication to this sacred duty
> Is total and wholehearted
> In the responsibility bestowed on me
> Never will I falter
> And with dignity and perseverance
> My standard will remain perfection.
> Through the years of diligence and praise
> And the discomfort of the elements
> I will walk my tour in humble reverence
> To the best of my ability.
> It is he who commands the respect I protect
> His bravery that made us so proud.
> Surrounded by well meaning crowds by day
> Alone in the thoughtful peace of night
> This soldier will in honored Glory rest
> Under my eternal vigilance.

The Caisson Platoon

One of the most impressive and memorable sights at Arlington National Cemetery is the full honor funeral in which the flag-draped casket of the deceased is solemnly borne to the gravesite on top of a horse-drawn caisson.

P. Bigler

Members of the caisson platoon harness the swing team in preparation for a full-honor funeral. Arlington is the only American cemetery that continues to use horses as a regular part of its funeral services

Like most American military funeral customs, this tradition traces its origins to the Civil War. At that time, an army artillery unit required massive support to sustain it during battle. Each gun was assigned a caisson for supply. These vehicles actually consisted of two tandem pieces — the limber, which was used to store additional ammunition, and the caisson itself, which was a flatbed wagon stocked with feed for the horses, additional supplies, extra rations, and even a spare wheel. The caissons were pulled by an allotment of six horses, all individually saddled and in harness so that they could quickly be deployed to replace those animals killed or wounded in battle. Likewise, when their supplies were removed, the caissons proved to be convenient ambulances to remove the battlefield wounded to the regiment's hospital or to cart off the dead for burial.

Arlington is the only national cemetery in the United States that continues to use horse-drawn caissons as a routine part of its military funerals. Full honor funerals are conducted on average twice per day, but the Caisson Platoon, Co. H, 3d US Infantry (the Old Guard), can accommodate up to six such burials.

There are thirty-three men assigned to the outfit — one warrant officer and thirty-two enlisted men. All of the men are volunteers and have been recruited from the ranks of the 3d Infantry because of their outstanding service records and their desire to work with horses. Three of the soldiers are experts in leather repair. They are responsible for making and maintaining all of the tack and harnesses used by the platoon. One soldier is a trained veterinary technician and another is an animal care specialist. The remainder of the soldiers are regular Army infantrymen.

When a soldier is first assigned to caisson duty, he undergoes three months of rigorous training before ever participating in a military funeral. During that time, he is expected to learn the anatomy of a horse and is instructed on how to detect and identify symptoms of disease. He is also taught how to ride both in-saddle and bareback on a variety of horses since each animal has a distinct personality and temperament. After the soldier is deemed competent, he is then trained to control two horses in-harness simultaneously. The soldier will be placed into funeral rotation as the lead rider only after these skills have been completely mastered. He is responsible for the caisson's front two horses (the lead team), which are generally the smallest and easiest to control animals. After six months of service, a soldier then advances to the middle pair of horses, the swing team which turns the caisson. Finally, after nine months with the platoon, he is assigned the wheel team, the most powerful and important horses since they are primarily responsible for stopping the caisson.

There are two caissons in daily use at Arlington Cemetery. Both were built in 1918 by the American Carriage and Foundry Co. to support 75-mm artillery pieces. These caissons, however, were quickly made obsolete by mechanized warfare during World War I and were scrapped, only to be salvaged for use at the cemetery.

The stables are located on post at Fort Myer. They house thirty-eight horses – a combination of black and gray. Teamed according to color, they are alternated each week. The stables are equipped with a fully operational blacksmith shop, which is responsible for shoeing all of the animals, a procedure required every six weeks.

Preparation for a full honor funeral takes a full five hours. The soldiers' assigned duty that day are to report to the stables each morning at 0400 hours. They must first pull the selected horses from their stalls, pick their hooves, and check their shoes. The animals then must be carefully trimmed, groomed, and washed. All of the tack must be prepared, the brass polished, and the McClellan saddles shined. Once these duties are completed, the horses are ready to be tacked up; the soldiers change into their dress Army uniforms complete with boots and spurs. Finally, the horses are bridled and hooked up to the caisson. After the soldiers saddle up, the section sergeant, who rides his own mount independently of the caisson, reads their orders. The funeral is finally conducted with appropriate ceremony and dignity.

Caparison Horse

For infantry officers of colonel rank and above, a caparison or riderless horse, follows the caisson to the gravesite. The black horse, the solemn color of mourning, has a sword strapped to its English riding saddle with boots reversed in the stirrups. The unmounted horse symbolizes the fact that the soldier will never ride again to lead his troops.

The current three caparison horses are named Pal Alto, Appomattox, and Maddy. They are never harnessed to a caisson but often serve additional duty as the section sergeant's mount. Although the custom of a riderless horse can be traced to ancient cultures, the first notable use of a caparison horse in the

"Black Jack" at the U.S. Capitol on November 25th, 1963. The McClellan saddle is equipped with a sword and boots reversed in the stirrups to signify a fallen leader.

United States occurred during the funeral of President Abraham Lincoln. During the final funeral procession in Springfield, Illinois, Lincoln's personal mount, Old Bob, was led behind the assassinated President's casket to the gravesite at the Oak Ridge Cemetery. The custom was later adopted by the armed services and expanded to include other high-ranking military officers.

The most famous caparison horse was Black Jack who was used during the funeral of President John F. Kennedy. A spry and skittish animal, the horse captured the nation's attention and seemed to epitomize the youth and vigor of the slain President. Black Jack was the last of the horses commissioned by the Quartermaster Corps. He served as a caparison horse in many other important funerals, including those of Dwight D. Eisenhower, Douglas MacArthur, Herbert Hoover, and Lyndon Johnson. Black Jack died at Fort Myer on February 6, 1976 at the advanced age of 29 years. He was buried on the post's parade grounds. The caisson platoon has since converted Black Jack's original stall into a museum honoring his historic service to the nation.

CHAPTER SIX

Your Sons and Daughters Have Served You Well

—Douglas MacArthur

The Tomb of the Unknown Soldier contributed to Arlington's growing stature as a national shrine, but as an operating cemetery, Arlington's primary appeal remained regional. By January 1, 1941, 49,927 people had been interred on the grounds but the onset of World War II was to forever transform Arlington due to the unique demands placed on the cemetery.

The United States entered World War II in December 1941 after the surprise Japanese attacks on American military and naval installations at Pearl Harbor, Hawaii, and the Philippine Islands. American soldiers were deployed throughout the Atlantic and Pacific theaters in a massive two-front effort to thwart ongoing German and Japanese aggression. As American combat troops began to sustain heavy casualties, new military cemeteries were hastily established abroad to accommodate the growing numbers of war dead. Over 93,000 U.S. soldiers were permanently interred in 14 new national cemeteries created on foreign soil. The vast majority of combat fatalities, however, were returned to the United States for burial in local cemeteries as specified by their surviving family members. During this period, Arlington increasingly became the preferred burial location for thousands of war dead. Interment levels swelled to an unprecedented annual rate of slightly over 2,000. The demand for grave space strained Arlington's limited land resources, and the need for increased burial capacity once again became the major problem facing cemetery officials. In February 1944, the Associated Press reported that, "At the present burial rate the capacity of Arlington Cemetery will be exhausted in five to seven years…only 14,000 more persons can be buried in Arlington. There are about 55,000 graves there now."

In response to the immediate crisis, the cemetery adopted a series of innovative policies designed to achieve maximum burial capacity. For the first time, the graves of minor children were located in a separate section, away from the plots of their parents since grave allotment for dependent burials required far less space. Likewise, new graves throughout Arlington were reduced from the traditional, generous and aesthetic 6 feet by 12 feet to a more crowded but much more utilitarian 5 feet by 10 feet. Interments were also permitted to within fifteen feet of roadways and the planting of new, large trees was radically curtailed to conserve valuable space. New interments were conducted throughout the cemetery in virtually all sections, including the older, more established areas without regard for any tract's historical era.

Foreign Nationals

Agreements concluded by the Allied powers required that host nations provide appropriate burial space for foreign military advisors and members of embassy delegations who died while on assignment in the United States during World War II. Eventually, 46 foreign nationals representing ten nations — Great Britain (24), Canada (4), France (4), Italy (4/2 POWs) the Netherlands (2), Germany (1 POW), Greece (1), South Africa (1), China (1), and later South Vietnam (2)—would be authorized burial at Arlington National Cemetery. Sir John Dill, the head of the British military mission in the United States and a co-planner of the D-Day invasion, was most notable in this group. Because of his importance, his grave is marked with an equestrian monument, one of only two in the cemetery.

During the war, the United States initiated a limited policy of transporting captured German and Italian soldiers to various states to assist American farmers with harvesting crops. On the eastern shore of Maryland, several farms took advantage of this much needed labor resource. Three prisoners died from illness during this time period and, in accordance with provisions of the Geneva Convention, were provided with appropriate military funerals in a nearby government cemetery. Since Arlington was the closest national cemetery to Maryland's eastern shore, it received the remains of the two Italian prisoners of war (Arcangelo Prudenza and Marlo Batista) and one German (Anton Hilberath) prisoner of war. All were interred on Section 15C near the Selfridge Gate. Every year on All Souls' Day, November 2, members of the Italian Embassy in Washington, D.C., continue to practice the Catholic custom of visiting the graves of the departed and decorating the simple graves of the two Italian soldiers.

Ignace Paderewski

Ignace Paderewski, renowned composer, famed pianist, and Polish nationalist, fled to the United States in December 1940, an unwilling exile from his native country, which had been overrun by the powerful Nazi war machine. Paderewski served as the President of the deposed Polish government and made persistent appeals to the American people to aid, supply, and liberate his besieged country.

On June 29, 1941, at the age of 80, Paderewski died in New York from natural causes. His last words were a patriotic prophecy, "Poland will rise again." With Poland still firmly under German occupation, the composer's remains could not be returned for burial to his native Krakow. After being informed of Paderewski's demise, President Franklin Roosevelt offered a temporary repose for the composer at Arlington Cemetery within the turret section of the Mast of the U.S.S. Maine memorial "...until Poland is free." The Polish Embassy gratefully accepted Roosevelt's proposal. Paderewski's remains were transported to Washington for an elaborate July 5 funeral service held in the Memorial Amphitheater. Afterwards, the casket was conveyed to the base of the Mast of the Maine where it was to be temporarily entombed. In 1944, the body of Manuel Quezon, the deposed president of the Philippines, was similarly allowed interment in the memorial until his nation was finally liberated from the Japanese. His remains were finally returned to his freed homeland after a return to peace.

Ironically, Paderewski's postwar repatriation never took place. Agreements reached at the Yalta conference in the winter of 1945 drastically altered the traditional political boundaries of Poland and provided the Soviet Union with the opportunity to install a communist-backed government. The Truman administration declared that Poland was not yet "free," the criterion for the return of Paderewski's body to Krakow. For the remainder of the Cold War, the composer's body continued to rest in the Mast of the Maine, hostage to international politics with no memorial or monument to indicate his presence.

Twenty years after Paderewski's death, the music critic for the Washington Post, Paul Hume, wrote an article which reported, "It is an anomaly probably unique in history that the body of a man who was worthy to be called 'perhaps the greatest living man' lies today in a tomb that is wholly without any marking of any kind to indicate his presence there." The column spawned a renewed interest in Paderewski and on May 9, 1963, President John F. Kennedy attended ceremonies near the Maine to dedicate a memorial plaque in honor of the composer. Kennedy reminded the gathered crowd of the reason for Paderewski's repose at Arlington, stating: "The understanding was that one day, when Poland would be free again, [Paderewski] would be returned to his native country. That day has not yet come. But I believe that in this land of the free, that Paderewski rests easily. We are proud to have him."

Six years later in 1969, the Archbishop of Krakow, Karol Wojtyla, visited Arlington National Cemetery and viewed the Polish composer's casket in the Maine memorial. A decade later, after Wojtyla's elevation to the papacy, he again returned to the United States as John Paul II. The Pope's visit to America led to a large amount of diplomatic activity concerning a possible return of Paderewski's remains to Poland should John Paul wish to escort the great composer's remains back to Krakow. However, the Pope was not able to include a visit to the cemetery in his itinerary. Shortly thereafter, the liberal Polish labor union, Solidarity, was brutally suppressed by the communist government that imposed an edict of martial law upon Poland. The political climate that had once favored the return of Paderewski's body quickly ended and would not be resurrected for several years.

As the 1980s came to a close, the world watched in amazement as Eastern Europe discarded forty years of Communist rule. In Poland, former shipyard worker and Solidarity leader, Lech Welesa, became the nation's prime minister. He quickly began to oust former Communists from his government. When he made a state visit to the United States in 1990, he visited Arlington and agreed that Paderewski's remains would be returned to Poland the following year, on the 50th anniversary of his death. It wasn't until June 1992, however, that the free Polish government was ready for the transfer. On June 27, the composer's remains were removed from the Maine memorial and escorted to Fort Myer for a service at the Memorial Chapel. A joint funeral procession then escorted the casket to the Memorial Gate where it was transported to Andrews Air Force Base to be flown back to Poland.

Some fifty-three years after the Nazis had forced Paderewski into exile, he received an enthusiastic welcome from his countrymen. President George Bush spoke at a funeral mass in Krakow and eulogized, "Today is truly a homecoming: the day Poland welcomes home a part of its proud history, a great patriot and patron of freedom." Paderewski was finally laid to rest in a free and independent Poland.

Iwo Jima Flag-Raisers

On February 19, 1945, the United States Marines landed on the small, volcanic island of Iwo Jima, located just 650 miles southeast of Tokyo. The Japanese resistance was fierce and continued for 36 days. The fighting eventually involved 75,000 American troops and cost a staggering 7,000 lives. An incredible 27 Medals of Honor were awarded for heroic actions on Iwo Jima, a measure of valor unprecedented in American military history.

During the early days of heavy fighting, members of the Fifth Marine Division were dispatched to scale the island's highest peak, Mount Suribaci. Once on the 550-foot summit, several Marines hoisted a small American flag. Because of the difficulty in seeing the colors, another group of six soldiers was organized and dispatched to replace the first flag with a larger, more evident one. The soldiers – PFC Ira Hayes, PFC Franklin Sousley, PFC Michael Strank, Pharmacist's Mate John Bradley, PFC Rene Gagnon, and Corporal Harlon Block – were photographed raising the flag by Associated Press cameraman, Joe Rosenthal. Throughout the United States, the dramatic photograph of the American flag-raising on Suribaci appeared in newspapers and magazines. It was subsequently adopted by the government as the official symbol for a forthcoming war bond drive.

The impact of the Rosenthal photograph led government officials to order removing the six soldiers who had participated in the flag-raising from combat so that they could represent the military services as official spokesmen

The Marine Corps Memorial located outside the northern entrance to Arlington Cemetery.
Three of the Iwo Jima flag-raisers are buried at the cemetery

in the crucial fund-raising effort. Three of the soldiers had already been killed in action, including PFC Michael Strank whose remains were eventually returned to the United States for burial at Arlington National Cemetery.

Two of the survivors, Ira "the Chief" Hayes and Rene Gagnon, were paraded throughout the United States during the war's final bond campaign and became somewhat reluctant symbols of American military valor. The flag-raising photograph evolved into an American icon and was converted into a best-selling postage stamp. Subsequently in 1954, it became the model for the new United States Marine Corps Memorial, which was constructed in Rosslyn just outside the northern entrance to Arlington National Cemetery.

Ira Hayes, a full-blooded Pima Indian from Arizona, suffered many personal reversals and died in 1955. He became the second of the Marine flag-raisers to be interred at Arlington Cemetery. Rene Gagnon, the last surviving member of the Iwo Jima contingent, experienced similar misfortunes until his death in October 1979. At the behest of his family, he was likewise buried at Arlington. His grave is located in Section 51 within just a few hundred yards of the Marine Corps Memorial. A brass relief of the Suribaci flag-raising was mounted on the reverse of his government headstone with the inscription:

For God and His Country
He Raised our Flag in Battle
And Showed a Measure of His
Pride at a Place Called "IWO JIMA"
Where Courage Never Died.

John J. Pershing

General of the Armies John J., "Black Jack," Pershing was confined to Walter Reed Army Hospital at the onset of World War II, physically unable

to contribute to the nation's war effort. The valiant commander of the American Expeditionary Forces (A.E.F.) during World War I was born just prior to the American Civil War in 1860. He attended the United States Military Academy at West Point and graduated in 1886. Pershing then served with the Army during the Indian campaigns against the Apache and Sioux tribes as well as in the Spanish-American conflict. He was sent to southwestern United States to apprehend the Mexican bandit, Francisco "Pancho" Villa, and with his forces, made several incursions across the border.

During this period, Pershing suffered a major personal tragedy when his wife and three daughters perished in a fire. Despite this loss, Pershing continued with his career and was placed in command of American forces destined for Europe. He steadfastly refused to allow dissolution of the AEF into separate commands under foreign generals and preached a doctrine of mobility. His strategy was successful in breaking the European stalemate by placing the Allied powers on the offensive and driving German troops from French soil.

At the conclusion of the war, to honor Pershing for his instrumental role in the victory, Congress promoted him to the rank of General of the Armies, a rank previously held only by George Washington. The act made Pershing the nation's highest ranking soldier, a position he held until his death in 1948 at the advanced age of 88 years.

The general had expressed a desire to be buried at Arlington National Cemetery, and he had personally selected a plot near the graves of many of the

U.S. Army Photo

soldiers he had commanded during the Great War. After lying in state in the U.S. Capitol, Pershing's coffin was then placed upon a horse-drawn caisson and transported to Arlington Cemetery on July 19, 1948. The caisson stopped on the plaza of the Memorial Amphitheater before the Tomb of the Unknown Soldier in tribute to the anonymous World War I soldier who undoubtedly had served under Pershing's command. A brief memorial service conducted in the Amphitheater was attended by President Harry S Truman. The procession then proceeded to the gravesite where Pershing was buried. A standard, white government headstone, virtually indistinguishable from the thousands of other American soldiers, was erected at his request. In 1968, in an adjoining grave, the general's grandson, second Lieutenant Richard Pershing, was buried after he was killed in action in Vietnam.

General Pershing wished to be buried among his men; a simple government headstone marks his grave. His grandson, Richard Pershing, was buried in an adjacent plot after he was killed in action in Vietnam.

Arlington in the 1950s

On December 1, 1951, John "Jack" Metzler was appointed the new superintendent of Arlington National Cemetery. A stern but well-respected administrator, Metzler immediately took control of the cemetery and began to investigate ways to improve its operation.

Despite the increased popularity of Arlington and the continued large number of interments, all graves were still being dug manually before Metzler's time. In 1955, he announced plans to automate the process and purchased two machines that were capable of, "open[ing] a grave in 12 minutes [while] a man with a shovel would take all day." In an interview with the *Washington Daily News* Metzler elaborated:

> 'The machine[s] also does a better job. The sides are smoother and the bottom of the grave is even. The machines dump the earth right into a truck, so the ground around the grave stays much cleaner...It costs around $29 to have a complete grave

done by hand,' he said. 'With the Trenchmaster we've now got the cost down to $9 plus change. No employees have been laid off because of the machines. They now have more time to maintain the cemetery's lawns and shrubs.'

The overall physical appearance of the cemetery was greatly enhanced during Metzler's stewardship of Arlington. Indeed, the superintendent took daily two-hour inspection tours of the grounds, covering the entire ten miles of the cemetery's roads. With an incredible eye for detail, Metzler would later deploy the cemetery's landscaping crew to key areas that required attention.

The 21 years Metzler remained superintendent were among the most critical in Arlington's history. In 1959, the cemetery completed its 100,000 interment, once again focusing attention on the traditional space problems at the cemetery. During the next decade, Metzler would be forced to implement a series of stringent eligibility requirements designed to restrict Arlington's burials. Likewise, he would be forced to ready the cemetery for its most notable burial, that of John F. Kennedy, the nation's assassinated Chief Executive.

CHAPTER SEVEN

The Torch Has Been Passed

—John F. Kennedy

Arlington National Cemetery always held special meaning for John F. Kennedy, the nation's thirty-fifth president. Dave Powers who formally held the position of White House doorkeeper but was, in fact, one of the President's closest friends and confidants, remembered: "Jack was very quiet...whenever he would go to Arlington Cemetery. He would think of the sacrifices that so many people had made," including that of his eldest brother, Joe, who was killed in the explosion of his airplane during World War II. It was a sacred place of burial for thousands of American veterans who had died for the nation's ideals.

On Armistice Day, November 11, 1961, John Kennedy made his first official visit to Arlington as President to place a wreath at the Tomb of the Unknown Soldier. At the conclusion of the brief ceremony, the President delivered the keynote address before an assembled crowd of 5,000 people in the Memorial Amphitheater. The address began:

> We meet in quiet commemoration of a historic day of peace. In an age that threatens the survival of freedom, we join together to honor those who made our freedom possible...It is a tragic fact, that war still more destructive and still more sanguinary followed [World War I]; that man's capacity to devise new ways of killing his fellow men have far outstripped his capacity to live in peace with his fellow man.

Noting the nation's commemoration of the American Civil War Centennial, President Kennedy acknowledged the cemetery's historic origin:

> This cemetery was first established ninety-seven years ago. In this hill were first buried men who died in an earlier war, a savage war here in our own country...These quiet grounds of this cemetery...remind us with pride of our obligations and opportunities. On this Veterans Day...let us pray...that there will be no

President John F. Kennedy's last visit to Arlington Cemetery, November 11, 1963, just eleven days before his assassination.

veterans of any further wars, not because all shall have perished but because all shall have learned to live together in peace. And to the dead here, in this cemetery, we say they are the race, they are the race immortal.

Two years later, just eleven days before his assassination, President Kennedy again returned to Arlington for the 1963 Armistice Day services. Accompanied by his playful 3-year-old son, John, Jr., the Presidential party was met by Major General Philip Wehle, Commander of the Military District of Washington. They were escorted to the Tomb for the traditional Presidential wreath-laying ceremony. Afterwards, Kennedy attended the scheduled memorial service in the Amphitheater but did not speak on this occasion. Dave Powers recalled that later, upon his return to the White House, the President was in a particularly somber mood and he shared a personal letter he had recently received from a retired Marine Corps major. The major had recently written to the President thanking him for saving the lives of several members of his company 20 years earlier while in the Solomon Islands. Serving at that time aboard PT-59, Lieutenant John Kennedy and his crew had made a daring rescue of a contingent of Marines who had been pinned down by heavy Japanese small arms fire on the island of Choiseul. One of the soldiers later died onboard the PT boat in Kennedy's personal bunk. The major's letter had served to make the President's Arlington visit particularly meaningful as a tangible reminder of the human toll of war.

November 22, 1963

On November 22, 1963, while on a political trip to Dallas, Texas, President Kennedy was shot and killed by an assassin. His sudden death shocked and stunned the nation for no one was prepared for the demise of the young, vibrant, 46-year old Chief Executive. Indeed, the Military District of Washington (M.D.W.), the agency entrusted with burial arrangements for high government officials, had prepared no contingency plans for a Kennedy funeral. Matters were further complicated by the fact that the President's widow, Jacqueline, had accompanied him to Dallas and her immediate burial wishes for the President were unknown.

Kennedy's brother-in-law and the director of the Peace Corps, Sargent Shriver, quickly arrived at the White House and began initial, tentative arrangements for the President's funeral. Lieutenant Colonel Paul Miller, the chief ceremonies officer at M.D.W., was summoned to the executive mansion and brought with him the relevant documents from the nation's last state funeral which had been conducted in 1958 for the Unknowns from Korea and World War II.

Among members of the Kennedy administration, it was privately assumed that the President's burial would take place in Brookline, Massachusetts. Precedent strongly supported this assumption since most American presidents were interred in their native states. (Among the notable exceptions are William Howard Taft, who is buried at Arlington, and Woodrow Wilson, who is interred at the National Cathedral in Washington, D.C.) Further supporting a New England burial had been the interment of President Kennedy's infant son, Patrick, just 15 weeks earlier after the newborn died from congestive heart and lung failure. Kennedy had last visited the child's grave while on a trip to Boston on October 19 and, on that occasion, remarked to Dave Powers that the boy seemed so forlorn there, buried all alone in the family plot. Thus, few intimates could conceive of the President being buried elsewhere. Jacqueline Kennedy likewise was reportedly to have remarked aboard Air Force One on the return from Dallas that: "...We'll bring them [Patrick and Jack] together, now," which was interpreted by many to confirm a Boston burial.

At 4:55 PM EST on November 22, 1963, the Associated Press teletype prematurely announced, "President Kennedy's body will lie in state at the White House tomorrow...There's nothing definite yet on the funeral, but it's understood it will be in Boston." The New York Times went to press later that day with the story, "The President was expected to be buried at the Kennedy family plot in Holyhood Cemetery, near Brookline, Mass. He is a native of Boston."

Shriver, however, had to prepare for all possibilities since the President's remains were still en route to Washington. He contacted the Superintendent of Arlington National Cemetery, Jack Metzler, to inquire about potential burial plots. Metzler informed Shriver that ample grave space was available for the President's burial. He also assured the President's brother-in-law that Arlington would be ready to honor their wishes should the Kennedy family decide upon a local interment. Immediately after the conversation, Metzler began to assemble the necessary staff who would be required to prepare for such an important funeral and ordered them to be available to work throughout the weekend.

The President's body finally arrived at Andrew's Air Force Base at 1800 hours. A contingent of military pallbearers led by Lieutenant Samuel Bird had been dispatched to remove the casket from Air Force One, but members of the Secret Service and the Presidential party refused to allow the soldiers near the remains. Instead, several members of the Kennedy administration struggled with the heavy, bronze coffin until they finally loaded it awkwardly into an awaiting Navy ambulance for transport to Bethesda Naval Hospital.

Since military physicians were to perform the required autopsy because of impending criminal charges, Shriver ordered Colonel Miller to assemble appropriate Armed Forces morticians to embalm and prepare the remains. Although military personnel were capable of the embalming procedure, the catastrophic nature of the President's wounds required the services of more skilled and experienced morticians. A private funeral home would have to be brought in to perform a cosmetic preparation of the body. Miller recommended Gawler's Funeral Home, one of the oldest and most widely respected funeral establishments in Washington. Shortly thereafter, the firm's undertakers were dispatched to Bethesda to await their grim task.

Finally, the White House staff received the first formal statement from Mrs. Kennedy concerning burial plans. Her only expressed wish was to model her husband's funeral after ceremonies rendered for Abraham Lincoln a century earlier. That evening, Professor James Robertson, the Executive Director of the United States Civil War Centennial Commission, was contacted by the White House and asked to complete the required research on the Lincoln burial. Robertson called David Mearns, the director of the Library of Congress, and arranged to meet him an hour later at the government repository.

The Library of Congress building had been routinely closed for the weekend and all of the office lights were inoperative since they were connected to a timer switch that prevented them from being used until the scheduled re-opening of the library the following Monday. Thus, armed only with flashlights, Robertson and Mearns descended into the stack areas, rummaging through the library's extensive holdings for pertinent copies of Frank Leslie's Illustrated and Harper's Weekly which graphically depicted the 1865 Lincoln funeral in detail. Once he located the relevant copies, Robertson took the material to the White House, and carpenters used the century-old drawings to transform the East Room with mourning crepe.

At Bethesda, the autopsy and the preparations of the President's remains were not fully completed until 0400 hours on November 23, 1963. A new, solid mahogany coffin had been purchased to replace the original bronze Dallas casket which had been damaged during the hasty return of the Presidential party to Washington. (The original casket was eventually disposed of at sea by orders of the Attorney General). Thirty minutes later, a Navy ambulance carrying the President's body slowly entered the White House grounds, saluted by members of a Marine honor guard detachment located along the North Portico entrance.

Lieutenant Bird and his six-member casket team moved forward and removed the President's coffin from the ambulance. According to military protocol, Bird was merely to supervise the transfer of the coffin, but the young Lieutenant quickly became aware that his team was having difficulty struggling under the enormous weight of the 1200-pound coffin. Ignoring military tradition, Lieutenant Bird stepped forward, grasped the end of the casket, and assisted his soldiers in conveying the remains into the East Room where the body was to lie in state while funeral arrangements were formalized.

November 23, 1963

Secretary of Defense Robert McNamara strongly believed that President Kennedy should be interred on federal property so that his grave would be readily accessible to the American people. At 0600, on Saturday, November 23, he contacted Superintendent Metzler and requested to see potential presidential burial locations at Arlington National Cemetery. Later that morning, McNamara was shown three potential plots – one near the Mast of the USS Maine, another at Dewey Circle, and finally one located on a slope directly below the Arlington House mansion. Shortly thereafter, Attorney General Robert F. Kennedy arrived at the cemetery and quickly eliminated the Dewey Circle plot as inaccessible and the Maine location as inappropriate. The gently sloping hill below the Custis-Lee Mansion, however, seemed to be an ideal tract since the grave would be positioned along a direct axis line between the Lincoln Memorial and Arlington House – a site that would forever link President Kennedy with his martyred predecessor, Abraham Lincoln, and to American history through Robert E. Lee.

The final decision on the grave was ultimately left to Mrs. Kennedy who came to the cemetery later that afternoon to see the plot. After carefully scrutinizing the area for over 15 minutes, the President's widow quietly nodded her assent and Metro Kowalchick, an Arlington employee, drove a tent stake into the ground to mark the approximate burial location.

Eugene H. Wilson, General Foreman of Field Operations at Arlington, remembered that the cemetery staff roped off the immediate area to prevent tourists and reporters from approaching the site. Ground crews then began the tedious task of removing mounds of leaves that had accumulated in the area. They also laid down cocomat runners and greens on the moist grass in preparation for the scheduled Monday services.

Once the cemetery was closed as scheduled to public visitation at 1700 hours, McNamara returned with Robert F. Kennedy to supervise the surveying of the grave. As the work was progressing, the two men walked up the hill to Arlington House. There, an employee with the National Park Service, Paul Fuqua, recounted that earlier that year, on March 3, President Kennedy and Charlie Bartlett had made an impromptu Sunday visit to the Custis-Lee mansion. After touring the house, Kennedy remarked that the view of Washington, D.C., was so magnificent that he could stay there forever – a statement that seemed to indirectly confirm the Arlington site as an appropriate location for the President's grave.

November 24, 1963

At 1230 hours, the President's flag-draped coffin was carried from the White House and placed upon a horse-drawn caisson for the procession to the Capitol Rotunda. Behind the caisson were the Presidential colors and the caparison horse, Black Jack, whose vacant saddle symbolized the demise of a fallen leader.

At the U.S. Capitol, Lt. Bird's joint service casket team, now augmented by two additional soldiers, removed the President's coffin from the caisson and carried it up the 36 steps into the Rotunda where it was carefully placed upon the Lincoln catafalque. A short memorial service was conducted and eulogies were delivered by Speaker John McCormack, Senator Mike Mansfield, and Chief Justice Earl Warren. Warren called John Kennedy, "a great and good President, the friend of all men of good will, a believer in dignity and equality of all human beings, a fighter for justice, an apostle of peace." Kennedy's successor, President Lyndon B. Johnson, placed a floral wreath before the coffin which was now guarded by a continual "Death Watch" of four soldiers.

For the remainder of the day and night, thousands of private citizens were allowed to enter the Capitol to pay their final respects to the nation's thirty-fifth president, some waiting for over 10 hours in the cold and dark for a brief moment of silent tribute.

That Sunday at Arlington, cemetery officials were attempting to dig the President's grave, but their efforts were continually hindered by the presence of gawking crowds and the news media. Metro Kowalchick remembered:

> We put up a plywood and canvas wall…We were trying to hide from the public, but the news media had rented helicopters and were flying overhead. We finished the sides [of the grave] with a long-handled shovel…We dug down seven feet, deep enough for Mrs. Kennedy to be buried there too. The soil was hard clay, there was a big oak tree. It's still there.

Mrs. Kennedy had expressed her desire earlier to mark the President's grave with an eternal flame similar to that of the French Unknown Soldier in Paris. It was difficult to devise such a complicated and potentially dangerous apparatus on short notice but the Army Corps of Engineers at Fort Belvoir was tasked with the job. After extensive deliberations, Colonel Clayton B. Lyle and his staff decided to fabricate a "luau-style" torch that would be fed by several propane gas tanks installed at the gravesite and covered with greens. The entire apparatus was designed, manufactured, tested and installed within 30 hours and worked flawlessly on the day of the funeral.

November 25, 1963

Lieutenant Bird was concerned about his casket team's performance. Although they had completed the Rotunda transfer perfectly and with dignity, the body bearers would be expected on Monday to carry the extremely heavy coffin down the Capitol steps, again at St. Matthew's Cathedral for the Catholic funeral Mass, and finally at Arlington Cemetery for the graveside services. The slightest error would be forever documented and, at worst, could disrupt the solemnity of the President's funeral. Bird, therefore, decided that his team would have to practice to fully ready themselves for the impending task.

Privacy for Bird's team was imperative, but reporters and newsmen were lurking throughout Washington, anxiously seeking an exclusive news story. Thus, it was decided to conduct the practice during the early morning hours at the Tomb of the Unknown Soldier which, along with the rest of Arlington, became a restricted military post once the cemetery had closed to the public. Futhermore, the site was ideal since there were numerous steps that would adequately simulate those of the Capitol and provide an ample challenge for the eight-member casket team.

Shortly after midnight on the morning of November 25, Bird's soldiers arrived at the Tomb. A casket used at Fort Myer during honor guard training exercises had been commandeered and filled with sandbags. For the next hour, Bird's body bearers repeatedly carried the coffin up and down the steps at the Tomb, sometimes with the Lieutenant and another soldier sitting on top to add weight. The two-hour drill successfully restored the casket team's confidence and the next day they performed magnificently.

Later that morning, virtually the entire nation watched the services for President Kennedy on television. At Arlington, however, cemetery employees conducted 23 other scheduled burials beginning with the burial of an Army colonel in Section 35 at 0900 hours. Each service was conducted with appropriate dignity and military honors including two interments which coincided with the 1500 hours state funeral for the President.

At the scheduled time, the long funeral procession entered the cemetery through the Memorial Gate. As the President's coffin was carried to the grave by Bird's casket team, members of the official funeral party gathered around the site some intermingling with military personnel and greatly hindering the precise execution of honor guard commands. The assembled crowd represented the greatest collection of dignitaries ever assembled at Arlington. Included among the mourners were President Charles de Gaulle of France, Chancellor Ludwig Erhard of the Federal Republic of Germany, Emperor Haile Selassie of Ethiopia, and Prince Philip of the United Kingdom. Overhead, 50 Navy and Air Force jets flew past the gravesite followed by the President's plane, Air Force One, which dipped its wing in final tribute.

At Mrs. Kennedy's request, a contingent of the Irish Guard stood opposite the grave and a Catholic committal service was performed by the Archbishop of Boston, Richard Cardinal Cushing. Cushing offered the prayer:

> Grant, O Lord, this mercy to Thy servant departed, that he who in his desires did Thy will may not receive the punishment of any misdeeds, and that as through faith that joined him to the company of the faithful here below, Thy mercy may make him the companion of the holy angels in heaven, through Christ our Lord, Amen.

A military firing party rendered honors which were followed immediately by the playing of "Taps." Army bugler, Sergeant Keith Clark, recalled, "I

Jacqueline Kennedy, clutching her husband's casket flag, leaves the gravesite with her brother-in-law, Robert F. Kennedy.

was to play immediately after the firing squad fired over my head. This added one more burden to my task as the extreme noise from the rifles left my ears ringing and, of course, that made my job that much more difficult as I had trouble hearing myself play. As many people know, I made the first bad note in my career…[but] many observers concluded I played the piece like that on purpose. One magazine article described my broken note as a 'French tear.'" Finally, the casket team adroitly folded the interment flag and Superintendent Metzler presented it to Mrs. Kennedy. The young widow, assisted by Robert F. Kennedy, then used a torch to light the eternal flame, thereby entrusting the President to the American people. Upon the completion of the formal serv-ices, several individuals lingered around the grave for a few moments, each silently saying good-bye to the President before departing the cemetery.

At 1532 hours, after members of the immediate family had left, the cas-ket was prepared to be lowered into the open grave. At that time, Superintendent Metzler was informed that members of the television news media were continuing to film and had ignored repeated requests to cease broadcasting. The lowering of a coffin is necessarily a logistical operation and is generally not seen by the public because the procedure would detract from the earlier, ceremonial parting achieved by the funeral service. Furious over the lack of cooperation from the media and intent upon maintaining privacy, Metzler ordered all electrical power shut off throughout the entire cemetery, thus effectively forcing the television networks off the air and allowing the casket to be privately lowered and the grave sealed.

The world's attention had been riveted on Arlington during the President's funeral services and almost immediately the cemetery was deluged with letters of condolence and tributes to the President, many simply addressed to "the Site of the Eternal Flame." Innumerable rosaries, prayer cards, and poems were mailed to the Kennedy family, including hundreds of efforts, frequently inaccurate, to memorialize Arlington as the President's bur-ial site. One representative tribute read:

> In eternal glory lie the mortal remains of our immortal President in Arlington National Cemetery.
> They rest on an open hillside among tall, bare elms, and a slight distance away stands a solitary cedar [sic].
>
> As one looks about from the grave of the President, one can see several hundred feet away thousands of our honored dead, and the floodlighted columns of the Curtis-Lee [sic] Mansion. One cannot help but sense a quiet, awesome feeling of deepest solem-nity pervading the cemetery grounds.
>
> At the head of his grave burns an Eternal Flame, and around it is a multi-array of flowers.

Let us trust that the light of this flame will cast its peaceful rays in the hearts of all men everywhere.

The Kennedy Gravesite

In accordance with Mrs. Kennedy's wishes, on December 4, 1963, the two deceased Kennedy children were reburied at Arlington – Patrick from Brookline, Massachusetts, and an unnamed daughter from Newport, Rhode Island. The *Washington Post* reported:

> Simple granite grave markers, taken from the original burial sites, have been erected for the two Kennedy children buried beside the late President Kennedy. To the right of the President's floral-banked grave is a small cross with the inscription 'Baby Girl Kennedy – August 23, 1956,' marking the spot of a stillborn child of the late President and Mrs. Kennedy. At the base of the cross are the words 'Suffer little children to come unto Me'. On the left side is a small marker with curved top for 'Patrick Bouvier Kennedy, Aug. 7, 1963 – Aug. 9, 1963' for the prematurely born baby, who died last summer.

R. Cramer

The Kennedy Memorial Grave was dedicated in March 1967. Around the ellipse are memorable quotations from the President's 1961 Inaugural Address.

The initial plot allotted for the President's grave was 20 feet by 30 feet and was completely enclosed by a white picket fence. Cemetery officials expected a large visitation at the grave initially but anticipated that tourism would slowly return to previous levels. During the first year, visitation at the Kennedy grave frequently reached 3,000 per hour and, on weekends, an estimated 50,000 people paid their respects daily. Incredibly, during the three years immediately following the President's death, 16 million people came to Arlington in what Superintendent Metzler called, "the most tremendous demonstration [of respect in history]."

The large increase in tourism at the cemetery had negative aspects as well. In 1964, the *Minneapolis Tribune* reported,

> So many visitors have been coming to the late President's grave that picturesque old Arlington cemetery has been struggling to maintain its dignity. The reason is that, unfortunately, not all the visitors are well behaved. Vandals are stealing flowers off other graves, picnickers leave mounds of litter, tombstones are resting places for the weary, and irreverent kids play leapfrog among the rows of granite. While one couple stood chatting in the line, their daughter worked a crayon over the tombstone of Oliver Wendell Holmes.
>
> 'Some people simply fail to appreciate what Arlington stands for,' says cemetery Supt. John C. Metzler. To him, 'Arlington is the shrine dedicated to the military, and it contains the history of our country engraved in granite.'

The temporary walkways leading to the grave were grossly inadequate and plans to build a more suitable gravesite were begun early in 1964. The architectural firm of John Warnecke and Associates was commissioned by the Kennedy family to design and build the new memorial grave. Construction began in 1965 and continued for two years, often with now Senator Robert F. Kennedy (D-NY) stopping at Arlington en route to his Capitol Hill offices to supervise the process.

On the night of March 14, 1967, President Kennedy and his two deceased children were secretly reinterred to the permanent grave which was located directly below the original burial location. The new site was formally blessed the following morning by Archbishop Cushing and the short service was attended by Mrs. Kennedy, Senators Robert and Edward Kennedy, and President Lyndon Johnson. The *Washington Post* provided the following account:

> Without previous announcement, the caskets of the 35th President and his two dead children were raised from their temporary sites last night, carried about 20 feet downhill and

reburied in the still uncompleted granite memorial. The 20-
minute [dedication] service today was conducted in a driving
rainstorm that pelted the participants as they huddled around
Cardinal Cushing, the archbishop of Boston…the service was
conducted at 7 a.m., about an hour before the cemetery opened
to the general public…At the conclusion of the private services,
Mrs. John F. Kennedy placed lilies of the valley on her husband's
grave.

The John F. Kennedy grave consists of Massachusetts granite quarried
over 150 years ago and was personally selected by members of the immediate
family. Sedum and fescue have been carefully planted between the stones to
achieve the impression of a natural, New England granite field. Along the
ellipse are inscribed several memorable quotations from President Kennedy's
1961 inaugural address. The entire area surrounding the grave was heavily
landscaped with numerous flowering trees planted in the immediate vicinity
to beautify the site.

The eternal flame remains the focal point of the memorial grave and successfully symbolizes the continued legacy of the President's ideals. His friend,
Dave Powers comments:

No matter how many times I would drive by, I found my eyes
attracted to that flame…and each time that I went by I said a
prayer for the President…[The Eternal Flame] is a reminder to
me of the greatest man I ever met and the best friend I ever
had…the shame of the assassination is what might have been
because today and tomorrow we shall miss him and we shall
never know for sure how different this world might have been
had fate enabled him to finish his agenda for peace.

Likewise, Melville Grosvenor, the editor of National Geographic eloquently wrote, "His life was such – the radiance he shed – that if we live to be
a hundred, we will remember how he graced this earth and how he left it…but
the deeds, the words, the examples of the man remain – and there will always
be a flame to remind us."

Robert F. Kennedy

On March 17, 1968, Robert F. Kennedy announced his own candidacy for
the presidency. The 42-year old New York Senator maintained that his decision to seek the nation's highest elective office was prompted primarily by the
military events in Vietnam. The conflict, he believed, was squandering
America's human and financial resources while diverting the nation's attention away from the more pressing domestic problems of poverty, unemploy-

ment, and racial discrimination.

During the following weeks, Robert Kennedy's campaign for the Democratic nomination gained momentum, greatly aided by President Lyndon Johnson's surprise decision not to seek reelection. On June 5, Senator Kennedy defeated Eugene McCarthy in the pivotal California primary and was now in an advantageous position to challenge Vice President Hubert Humphrey for the Democratic nomination at the Chicago convention scheduled for later that summer. Shortly after delivering a triumphal speech to a group of campaign workers at the Ambassador Hotel in Los Angeles, he was shot and seriously wounded by a young Palestinian, Sirhan Sirhan, who opposed the Senator's outspoken support for the state of Israel.

Bobby Kennedy clung to life for the next 24 hours, but despite heroic life-saving efforts and emergency surgery, the head wound he sustained proved fatal and the Senator died on June 6. His body was flown to New York City where it laid in state at St. Patrick's Cathedral on Fifth Avenue.

When informed of Kennedy's demise, Arlington Cemetery officials did not anticipate that the Senator would be buried at the cemetery since a series of more rigorous eligibility requirements had been implemented just the previous year. However, further investigation proved that Kennedy was, in fact, qualified for interment at Arlington as a former cabinet official with prior military service. Family members soon requested that he be buried in a plot adjacent to the John Kennedy grave since the two brothers had been virtually inseparable during their lives. However, the Senator's widow, Ethel, requested that military participation in the services be held to a bare minimum.

The funeral Mass for Bobby Kennedy was conducted at St. Patrick's Cathedral on Saturday, June 8. It was attended by over 2,000 people, including all the major presidential contenders – Eugene McCarthy, Hubert Humphrey, and Richard Nixon. In the most memorable and moving address of his career, Senator Edward Kennedy eulogized:

> My brother need not be idealized, or enlarged in death beyond what he was in life, to be remembered simply as a good and decent man, who saw wrong and tried to right it, saw suffering and tried to heal it, saw war and tried to stop it.
>
> Those of us who loved him and who take him to his rest today pray that what he was to us and what he wished for others will some day come to pass for all the world.
>
> As he said many times, in many parts of this nation, to those he touched and who sought to touch him: 'Some men see things as they are and say why. I dream things that never were and say why not.'

At the conclusion of the service, the Senator's casket was placed aboard a special train for transport back to Washington, D.C., for the committal services at Arlington. The twenty-one car funeral train was scheduled to pass through the major East Coast cities of Newark, Camden, Philadelphia, and Baltimore, analogous to the journey of the Lincoln funeral train of a century earlier. The Senator's coffin was carefully positioned on a platform in the last car so that it could be seen by the thousands of expected mourners with a member of the Kennedy family maintaining a constant vigil.

No one anticipated the huge outpouring of grief that became apparent as the train slowly passed through New York. Thousands of people quietly gathered along the tracks to glimpse the Senator's coffin, many weeping while others passively held small American flags. Tragically, in Elizabeth, New Jersey, a large group of people failed to see an approaching northbound train and, in the ensuing panic, two people were struck by the oncoming train and instantly killed. Informed of the horrible accident, the Kennedy family ordered their train further slowed and all northbound traffic between Washington and New York was stopped.

Aboard the funeral train were over 700 people, including Senator Kennedy's pregnant widow and his ten children. The atmosphere was that of an Irish wake where, in Theodore White's words, "[the mourners attempt to] make a man come alive again in the affection and memory of his friends."

The train was by now hopelessly behind schedule and did not arrive at Washington's Union Station until 2110 hours, having required 8 1/2 hours to make the 225-mile journey from New York. By now, darkness was descending upon the nation's capital and Arlington was forced to begin preparations for an unprecedented nighttime funeral. Floodlights had been commandeered and strategically deployed around the open grave. Military personnel had obtained 1,500 candles from nearby St. Matthew's Cathedral for the expected mourners.

The funeral procession formed at the train station and Senator Kennedy's casket was removed by thirteen civilian pallbearers, including former astronaut John Glenn, former Secretary of Defense Robert McNamara, family friend Maxwell Taylor, Robert's eldest son Joe Kennedy, and the sole surviving brother, Senator Edward Kennedy. The motorcade route was designed to pass by all of the significant government buildings in Robert Kennedy's political career including the U.S. Capitol and the Department of Justice. When the procession reached the Lincoln Memorial, the Senator's hearse paused briefly while the Marine Corps band played "The Battle Hymn of the Republic" as hundreds of civil rights protestors from the adjacent Resurrection City encampment silently looked on.

Finally the motorcade arrived at the gravesite at 2030 hours. There, the casket was bourne to the gravesite by the pallbearers and a brief 15-minute service, illuminated only by floodlights and the flickering candles of the mourners, was conducted by Archbishop Terrence Cook. At the conclusion of the ceremony, the interment flag was carefully folded by John Glenn and presented to the Senator's widow by her eldest son, Joe.

The grave of Robert F. Kennedy was marked with a simple, white Christian cross and was initially located only about 20 feet from the grave of the President. A more suitable and elaborate memorial was desired by family members and the architect I.M. Pei, who would later design the East Wing of the National Gallery of Art and the John F. Kennedy Library, was commissioned to devise drawings for the new grave.

In 1971, construction was completed on the memorial grave and Robert Kennedy's remains were reinterred to their present site, still adjacent to the grave of the John Kennedy. A Christian cross marks the grave and along the fountain area are inscriptions from two of Robert Kennedy's most notable speeches including his eloquent and poignant eulogy to Martin Luther King delivered in Indianapolis on April 4, 1968. Each year, the graves of both Robert and John Kennedy are visited by over four million people.

Jacqueline Kennedy Onassis

In January 1994, Jacqueline Kennedy Onassis learned from her doctors that she had contracted non-Hodgkin's lymphoma. Despite aggressive treatment, the former First Lady died from her illness a few months later on May 20 at the age of 65. The following day, Arlington National Cemetery officials were notified of the family's desire for an interment at the Kennedy gravesite. Plans were immediately begun for a private committal service and the gravesite was closed to public visitation over the weekend to prepare the crypt.

On Monday, May 23, a funeral Mass was conducted in New York City after which the casket was flown to Washington, D.C., where a motorcade awaited. The solemn procession arrived at Arlington at 1:40 in the afternoon on a blistering hot May day. President Bill Clinton greeted the surviving Kennedy children – Caroline Kennedy Schlossberg and John F. Kennedy, Jr. – as their mother's casket was carried to the gravesite by eight civilian pallbearers. There, an intimate and private service was conducted with readings from the New Testament and 121st Psalm. A television crew was positioned a discreet distance away to allow for pool coverage to the nation.

When the gravesite reopened the following morning, thousands of people quietly made their way to the site, some patiently waiting for over two hours to pay their final respects. A few weeks later, a bronze memorial plaque was added to the grave. It read:

Jacqueline Bouvier Kennedy Onassis
1929 - 1994

CHAPTER EIGHT

May God Cradle You in His Loving Arms

—Ronald Reagan

Despite the massive efforts to conserve grave space during the previous two decades, it was apparent that Arlington would still be forced to cease burial operations by the late 1960s unless even more drastic policies were implemented. In 1961, Arlington became the first national cemetery to abolish the traditional practice of side-by-side interments for family members and adopted an experimental tier burial policy. An eligible veteran, spouse, and all dependents were allotted a single grave with burials accomplished through stacking or offsetting the various coffins. The tier system instantly doubled Arlington's existing burial capacity and soon proved so efficient that the practice was mandated for the entire national cemetery system the following year.

In 1967, to supplement the tier system, other grave conservation efforts were also adopted at Arlington. The Army imposed a series of stringent eligibility requirements that severely restricted in-ground burial to only a select number of servicemen. The controversial new criteria allowed interment for only those who died while on active duty; individuals who qualified for retirement benefits; Medal of Honor recipients; holders of the Distinguished Service Cross, the Silver Star, the Purple Heart, or comparable decorations; and spouses and dependents of the same.

The immediate need for additional space was alleviated somewhat when the cemetery made its most important land acquisition in 1966. The Fort Myer South Post was formally ceded to Arlington to expand the cemetery's grave facilities. The military installation, which adjoined Arlington's eastern boundary, encompassed 190 acres of land. Its dilapidated World War II-era buildings were quickly razed while extensive landscaping was undertaken to beautify the area to prepare it for future burials. With the addition of the South Post acreage, Arlington's size swelled to 612 acres, ensuring the continued operation of the cemetery well into the next century.

Vietnam

For most Americans, the image of the Vietnam conflict was restricted to

graphic scenes of combat televised during the evening news. Arlington, however, was daily experiencing the tangible human residue of that conflict.
During the late 1960s when American forces were sustaining well over 500
combat-related fatalities weekly, interments at Arlington correspondingly
increased. Thurman Higginbotham, who worked as a cemetery representative
during the war, remembered that the six-member interment staff was routinely handling between 30 and 37 burials daily. On one occasion, the cemetery
performed an unprecedented 47 funerals, a level never again duplicated.

The Vietnam Conflict never gained the complete support of the
American people and, as casualties began to mount, funeral services for those
killed in the war were commonly marred by bitterness. Young widows, parents,
and relatives of the deceased, overcome with grief over their loss, frequently
refused to accept the triangular folded casket flags. Some bereaved families
severely restricted military participation in the services.

Relatives of many servicemen who were missing-in-action or whose
remains were never recovered from Vietnam were allowed to erect small government memorial stones to their loved ones. Each marker begins with the
identical inscription, "In Memory of..." Over 2,000 servicemen remained
unaccountable after the Vietnam Conflict and entire new sections reserved
for the bodiless graves had to be created marked only by such cenotaphs.

While Arlington was attempting to conduct an unprecedented number of
funerals, visitation levels had simultaneously peaked after the interment of
President John F. Kennedy. The cemetery remained open to civilian traffic
and, on some days, over 5,000 cars and buses would routinely drive through
the cemetery, clogging roads and frequently interfering with ongoing funeral
processions. A study commissioned by the Department of the Army reported,
"Auto congestion, noisy buses within the gates, and tourists in holiday mood
contradict the atmosphere of dignity and repose." In 1970, in an effort to
respect the grief of families in mourning and to preserve the cemetery's tran-
quil dignity, Arlington was permanently closed to private vehicular traffic.

The *U.S.S. Forrestal*

The United States began its heaviest bombing raids of the war against
major military targets in North Vietnam in 1967. The carrier, U.S.S. *Forrestal*,
was dispatched for the first time to the Tonkin Golf to provide additional
planes for the air strikes. On July 29, while the *Forrestal* was in the process of
launching several heavily armed aircraft, one of the plane's jet exhausts ignited a missile on a nearby fighter, exploding a fully loaded auxiliary fuel tank.
The fire quickly spread throughout the flight deck and below deck compart-
ments, detonating tons of ammunition.

The 4,300 men of the *Forrestal* crew heroically battled the intense flames
for over 14 hours while escort destroyers moved precariously to within 10 feet
of the burning carrier to spray thousands of gallons of water on the flames.

U.S. Navy Photo

In 1967, a missile exploded on the U.S.S. Forrestal. Eighteen members of the crew were buried in a group grave at Arlington.

The heavily damaged *Forrestal* limped slowly back toward port in the Philippines while the crew began the gruesome task of accounting for missing sailors. The *Washington Post* reported:

> Some [Navy personnel] were burned to ashes fighting the blaze or trying to escape from their burning planes. Some were blown into the sea by bomb explosions and others are sealed in compartments below the flight deck where they were sleeping when the fire began...Crewmen continued to search the 76,000-ton carrier for bodies, hacking through bulkheads and wading through water-filled passageways still warm from the flames of the burning fuel that poured down openings into the lower decks of the ship.

Twenty-one jet aircraft had been destroyed in the fire and an additional 42 were heavily damaged. It was the worst combat related naval disaster since World War II with 129 men killed. Eventually, 18 of the deceased were buried at Arlington Cemetery in Section 46. Since their remains were burned beyond recognition, they were interred together in a common grave with a single headstone bearing the inscription "Died in Fires and Explosions – U.S.S. *Forrestal*, July 29, 1967."

The U.S.S. *Liberty*

The intelligence ship U.S.S. Liberty listing badly after a combined missile and torpedo assault by Israeli forces during the 1967 Arab-Israeli War.

In June 1967, an unarmed intelligence ship, the *U.S.S. Liberty*, was dispatched to the Middle East to monitor the ongoing communications between belligerents during the Arab-Israeli War. While in international waters and conspicuously displaying the American flag, the *Liberty* was repeatedly attacked by heavily armed Israeli jet fighters with missiles and napalm.

Virtually defenseless, the American vessel desperately radioed for assistance from the U.S. Sixth Fleet. The carrier America dispatched four combat-ready F-4 fighters to the scene. When Secretary of Defense McNamara was informed that the American planes were equipped with nuclear weapons, the aircraft were immediately recalled, leaving the Liberty to weather the ongoing assault alone.

The attack on the *Liberty* was joined by two Israeli patrol boats while the ship's officers and sailors, unaware of the developments involving the America, anxiously awaited air support. A torpedo hit the vessel's starboard side and ripped a 40-foot hole in the ship's hull, instantly killing 25 members of the crew.

Several hours after the incident, the Israeli government sent apologies to the United States, claiming that the *Liberty* had been mistakenly identified as a potentially hostile vessel. In a subsequent formal notification delivered to the American government, Israel stated, "its since expression of deep regret for the tragic accident in which, at the height of hostilities in the area, the U.S.S. *Liberty* was hit by Israeli fire."

Israel eventually paid $3.5 million in reparation to the families of the 34 American sailors who were killed and a similar sum to the 171 wounded servicemen. Inexplicably, the United States seemed content to dismiss the attack and accept the Israeli version of the incident while virtually ignoring the testimony of the *Liberty* officers and men that proved conclusively that the attack on the ship was both deliberate and premeditated. In his memoirs written four years after the event, President Lyndon Johnson inaccurately summarized the entire episode: "Ten men of the *Liberty* crew were killed and a hundred were wounded [sic]. This heartbreaking episode grieved the Israelis deeply, as it did us...Aside from the tragic accident involving the *Liberty*, no American died in the Middle East war in 1967."

The remains of 14 members of the *Liberty* crew, including the ship's Executive Officer, LCDR Philip Armstrong, were taken to Arlington National Cemetery for burial. Three of the bodies were individually unidentifiable and were thus buried under a group headstone listing the names of the six missing servicemen of the *Liberty* crew. Philip Ennes in his book, *The Assault on the* Liberty, recounts, "Three men, apparently swept away and into the sea, could not be accounted for. Three others could not be identified. These were eventually buried, along with stray limbs and other unidentifiable parts, in a mass grave at Arlington National Cemetery."

The group marker was originally engraved with the terse inscription "Died in the Eastern Mediterranean." After years of petitioning, the United States Navy agreed to provide a more appropriate epitaph. The new headstone was finally erected in October 1982, 15 years after the original incident.

In his address during the unveiling ceremonies Commander X. Bender Tansill explained:

> The new headstone carries this epitaph – 'Killed – U.S.S. *Liberty*-June 8, 1967.' We now know that these six crewmen were killed. Perhaps it would have been better to have included the words 'in combat' but now we know from the epitaph that they were killed on the U.S.S. *Liberty*, they did not just die in an Eastern Sea...These five sailors and one Marine did not just die! They were deliberately killed on board of the U.S.S. *Liberty* when that ship of our Navy was intentionally attacked without warning...These six crewmen were blown to pieces when the torpedo struck the U.S.S. *Liberty* and blew a hole in it, 40 feet long below the waterline.

Audie Murphy

The July 16, 1945, cover of Life magazine featured "The Most Decorated Soldier" of World War II, Audie Murphy. As a boy from Farmville, Texas, Murphy had lied about his age in 1942 to enlist in the United States Army as a private. During the military campaigns in Sicily, Italy and Germany, he was rapidly promoted to the rank of Second Lieutenant for his valorous battlefield conduct and was awarded 24 decorations including the nation's highest, the Congressional Medal of Honor. The accompanying citation detailed Murphy's bravery while in Germany:

> With [6] enemy tanks abreast of his position, 2d Lieutenant
> Murphy climbed on [a] burning tank destroyer, which was in
> danger of blowing up at any moment, and employed its .50 cal-
> iber machine gun...his deadly fire killed dozens of
> Germans...[Murphy] received a leg wound, but ignored it and
> continued the single-handed fight until ammunition was
> exhausted...2d Lieutenant Murphy's indomitable courage and
> his refusal to give an inch of ground saved his company from pos-
> sible encirclement and destruction, and enabled it to hold the
> woods which had been the enemy's objective.

After the war and his release from the Army, Murphy published an auto-
biographical account of his war experiences entitled, To Hell and Back,
which was adapted by Hollywood into a feature-length drama in which
Murphy portrayed himself. Murphy went on to star in 40 motion pictures
during his acting career but a failed marriage and financial difficulties tar-
nished his reputation. His life ended tragically in 1971 when the small private plane in which he was traveling crashed in the Blue Ridge Mountains
of Virginia.

The United States Army accorded its most decorated soldier a funeral
with full military honors at Arlington National Cemetery. The graveside
services were attended by the United Nations Ambassador, George H.W.
Bush, officially representing President Richard Nixon. In an official proclamation, the President's honored Audie Murphy:

> [Audie Murphy] came to epitomize the gallantry in action of
> America's fighting men...When challenged to defend their
> freedom, Americans have always stood ready to defend it with
> courage and daring, and each war in which the nation has been
> engaged has produced its own special heroes...As America's
> most decorated hero of World War II, Audie Murphy not only
> won the admiration of millions for his own brave exploits, he
> also came to epitomize the gallantry in action of American
> fighting men. The nation stands in his debt and mourns at his
> death.

Audie Murphy's grave is situated in the immediate vicinity of the
Memorial Amphitheater. Shortly after his burial, several proposals were sub-
mitted for a more elaborate memorial at the Arlington gravesite, many bor-
dering on ostentation. Murphy's widow, however, tastefully refused all such
plans and consented only to a modest walkway leading to her husband's simple grave, marked at her behest with a white government headstone.

The Bicentennial

Raymond J. Costanzo, a World War II veteran and POW who had served with the 508 Parachute Infantry, 82nd Airborne Division during the Normandy invasion, was appointed the new superintendent of Arlington Cemetery on May 18, 1975. His first major task was to ready the cemetery for the forthcoming Bicentennial celebrations commemorating the 200th anniversary of the founding of the United States.

A much-needed renovation of the Memorial Amphitheater was undertaken to accommodate the numerous tourists and foreign visitors expected to come to Arlington during the Bicentennial year. Repairs to the structure and the addition of facilities for the handicapped were completed. To enhance the physical appearance of the cemetery, Costanzo also established a rigorous and ongoing policy of straightening and realigning of headstones while the overall maintenance and landscaping of the grounds were greatly improved.

During 1976, virtually every major head of state from the free world, including Queen Elizabeth of Great Britain, King Juan Carlos of Spain, and Emperor Hirohito of Japan, visited the United States and paid honor to American veterans by placing a wreath at the Tomb of the Unknown Soldier.

The Veterans' Administration approved new government headstones inscribed with gold leaf lettering to specifically honor deceased Medal of Honor recipients during the nation's celebrations. Throughout Arlington, all of the headstones of Medal of Honor recipients were replaced with the new Bicentennial markers. Only Audie Murphy's grave was excepted at the behest of his widow who declined a replacement stone.

Also during the Bicentennial, Costanzo created a Historian's Office to document the various services and ceremonies conducted at the cemetery. The superintendent remembers that "...bits and pieces of historical documents...[had] been gathering dust, rolled up in somebody's drawer...[and] getting it put into some type of order [was a major priority.]" Thus, the office began a preservation program to safeguard many of Arlington's priceless artifacts.

When the historians began the massive task of gathering and organizing the cemetery's extensive historical documents and records, they discovered that Arlington's original burial records, dating from 1864, had been stored in an unused crypt under the colonnade at the Memorial Amphitheater. Among some of the other items discovered were several volumes documenting the interment of African-American citizens from the post-Civil War Freemen's Village and the 1963 funeral scheduling book that contained important information concerning the cemetery's planning for the burial of President John F. Kennedy. All of the volumes were suffering from the damaging effects of moisture and mold which, if left unchecked, could destroy the irreplaceable volumes. The Superintendent, after being informed of the situation, authorized the construction of a new storage facility with controlled temperature and humidity to house the collections. A rare book expert from the Library of Congress was consulted to assess the damage to the material. He was eventually commissioned to begin the delicate restoration and preservation of the volumes.

Hostage Rescue Mission

In 1979, the recently deposed Shah of Iran entered the United States to seek medical treatment for cancer. His visit spurred Islamic fundamentalists to storm the American Embassy in Teheran where they seized 53 American citizens whom they held hostage while demanding the Shah's return to his native country. The Carter administration attempted to negotiate the release of the Americans. After months of frustrating and futile deliberations with the Ayatullah Khomeini's revolutionary government, the President approved a dramatic plan to rescue the American captives.

For four months, 180 American servicemen secretly practiced the intricate and precise maneuvers that would be required to land an American commando force deep in Iranian territory in an effort to liberate the hostages. When the plan was finally implemented on April 25, 1980, a series of unfortunate accidents doomed the mission to failure.

Eight helicopters and six C-130 transport planes were first scheduled to rendezvous at a predetermined desert location 250 miles east of the Iranian capital. Two of the helicopters were unable to reach their destination after being disabled by a sudden desert sandstorm. A third craft developed hydraulic problems shortly after landing in the staging area and was unable to proceed to Teheran. With the rescue operations requiring a minimum of six fully operational helicopters, mission commanders wisely decided to abort the rescue. While attempting to refuel for a return to their respective bases, one of the helicopters crashed into a transport plane, exploding and killing eight men. Fearing detection, the remainder of the force was quickly loaded on board the remaining planes and flown out of Iran. The following day, the Iranian government photographed the disaster area. The charred remains of the eight American servicemen were taken to Teheran and placed on public display where they were desecrated and their remains commingled by angry mobs.

President Carter sadly announced the failure of the mission and fully accepted blame for the incident, "It was my decision to attempt the rescue operation. It was my decision to cancel it when problems developed. The responsibility is fully my own."

On May 9, President Carter attended memorial services at Arlington National Cemetery for the eight servicemen who had been killed in the mission. In an address to the mourners, Carter quoted Robert E. Lee stating, "Duty is the sublimest word in our language. Do your duty in all things. You cannot do more, you should never do less." He went on to praise the courage of the American servicemen. One of the mourners later recalled that Major Richard Bakke, U.S.A.F., one of the pilots killed during the mission, "…looked forward with enthusiasm and anticipation to this last opportunity to serve not for the glory it offered but for the deep satisfaction of defending that which is good and decent."

Several weeks later, the bodies of the eight Americans were returned to the United States. The remains of Major Bakke, Major Harold Lewis, U.S.A.F., and TSG Joel Mayo, U.S.A.F., were individually unidentifiable and were consigned to a single coffin and buried at Arlington National Cemetery in Section 46 near the Memorial Amphitheater. A white marble monument with a bronze memorial plaque was erected nearby in 1983 in tribute to all of the men who died in the noble effort to rescue the American hostages.

U.S. Army Photo

Boxing greats Muhammad Ali, Sugar Ray Leonard, and Joe Frazier attend a 1986 memorial service at the grave of Heavyweight Champion Joe Louis.

Joe Louis

Joe Louis won the heavyweight championship in 1937 and held the boxing title longer than any other individual, forfeiting it only upon retirement in 1949. Known in the ring as the "Brown Bomber," Louis' boxing career spanned 71 fights and included 25 title defenses.

At the onset of World War II, Louis volunteered for service in the United States Army. He served in both North Africa and Europe where he fought exhibition bouts before Allied troops, eventually appearing before over 2 million soldiers. At the conclusion of the war, TSG Louis was awarded the Legion of Merit for his contributions to the American war effort.

Louis died on April 12, 1981, but despite his wartime military service, he remained ineligible for in-ground burial at Arlington. President Ronald Reagan quickly waived the requirements and authorized Louis' interment at the cemetery.

On April 21, interdenominational funeral services were conducted for Joe Louis at Arlington National Cemetery. In attendance were fellow heavyweight champions, Muhammad Ali, Joe Frazier, and Joe Walcott, as well as the Reverend Jesse Jackson and Secretary of State Caspar Weinberger. President Reagan, still recuperating from wounds suffered during an assassination attempt, sent a letter to be read at the services: The President's stated:

> [I] was privileged and grateful to have had Joe Louis as my friend...out of the ring, he was a considerate and soft spoken man. Inside the ring, his courage, strength, and confident skill wrote a unique and unforgettable chapter in sports history. But Joe Louis was more than a sports' legend. His career was an indictment of racial bigotry, and a source of pride and inspiration to millions of white and black people around the world.
>
> The champion's son, Joe Louis Barrow, Jr., eulogized his father:
>
> It's wonderful that we're here at the National Cemetery, where you will finally rest, because you were a patriot, your served the country well, you provided it with the guidance and the faith it needed at a time when the country was down and the people needed a lift...You looked at me [during the Vietnam War] and you said 'This is a beautiful country, son, and it's most important that we stand by it. It may make mistakes. It may not be exactly right, but we have to stand by it.' We are going to miss you an awful lot because you were the greatest, truly the greatest.

Joe Louis' grave is located in section 7A, just below the Tomb of the Unknown Soldier.

Matthew Henson

Famed Arctic explorer Robert E. Peary was buried with full military honors at Arlington shortly after his death in 1920. Two years later, the National Geographic Society erected a more suitable memorial at the Peary gravesite to commemorate his claim as being the first person to reach the North Pole. The monument was carved from white Maine granite and features a detailed globe with the seven continents in low relief. A bronze star marks the precise location of the North Pole. Inscribed on its base in Latin is the motto, "I will find a way or make one."

During the ensuing years, one of the more frequent visitors to the Peary grave was his longtime friend and collaborator, Matthew Henson. The two originally met in 1887 in a Washington, D.C. clothing store where Henson worked as a stock clerk. Peary initially enlisted Henson for an expedition to Nicaragua to survey possible sites for a Central American canal.

After their return, Peary began plans for exploring the Arctic in a quest to be the first person to reach the North Pole. Henson became an integral part of all such expeditions and an expert dog-sled driver, skilled hunter, and avid explorer. He learned the Eskimo language fluently and, because of his dark skin, he was welcomed by the

Arctic Explorer Matthew Henson shortly after being the first African-American to reach the North Pole. Henson placed the American flag at the Pole in 1909 during Robert Peary's expedition.

native inhabitants as a brother. In his 1910 book on the North Pole expeditions, Peary wrote of Henson, "I have taken him with me on each and all of my northern expeditions...and almost without exception on each of my 'farthest' sledge trips. This position I have given him, primarily because of his adaptability and fitness for work; secondly on account of his loyalty. He has shared all the physical hardships of my Arctic work. His is now about forty years old, and can handle a sledge better, and is probably a better dog-driver, than any other man living, except some of the best of the Eskimo hunters themselves."

Despite several failed attempts to reach the Pole, Peary and Henson continued to persevere. Together they braved dangerous ice floes, fuel shortages, frigid temperatures, dense fog, and unpredictable Arctic leads until they finally reached their goal on April 6, 1909. Henson was given the honor of placing the Stars and Stripes at the Pole.

When news of their feat finally reached the United States, Peary was hailed as a national hero but Henson

The grave of Matthew Henson adjacent to that of his colleague, Robert Peary. Henson was re-interred to Arlington National Cemetery in 1988 in recognition of his status as "Co-discoverer of the North Pole."

received little credit. He eventually moved to Harlem and was forced to accept a menial job in a Bronx garage. Later he became a messenger with the U.S. Customs Service. Efforts to award Henson a pension for his Arctic exploits were consistently thwarted in Congress as was legislation initiated in the 1950s to award him the Medal of Honor. Upon his death in 1955, he was buried in the Woodlawn Cemetery in the Bronx. A small, inconspicuous granite headstone was all that marked his grave, modestly inscribed with the statement, "Reached the North Pole with Peary."

In 1986, Professor Allen Counter of Harvard University began an intensive lobbying campaign to recognize Henson's contributions to Peary's polar expeditions. He requested that Henson's remains be reinterred in Arlington National Cemetery to an area near the Peary gravesite. After several bureaucratic delays, President Ronald Reagan finally granted an exemption form the cemetery's rigorous burial restrictions and authorized Henson's burial at Arlington.

On April 6, 1988, 79 years after reaching the Pole, Henson's remains along with those of his wife were buried at Arlington with military honors in a grave directly adjacent to that of Robert Peary's. A five-foot granite marker was unveiled with an impressive bronze plaque featuring Matthew Henson at the North Pole along with his four Eskimo companions – Egingwah, Ootah, Ooqueah, and Seegloo. The memorial belatedly credits Matthew Henson as the "Co-discoverer of the North Pole."

Terrorism

Americans were the repeated targets of terrorist attacks during the 1980s with United States citizens murdered in Central America, Asia, and the Middle East. The greatest loss of life during this bloody decade occurred in Lebanon.

The turmoil in Lebanon was caused by warring religious factions and further threatened the precarious balance of peace in the Middle East. In as effort to bring stability to the region, an international peace mission was established consisting of military contingents from France, Italy, Britain, and the United States. Over 1,600 members of the Eighth Marine Regiment were assigned to the Beirut International Airport but were subjected to constant sniper fire from neighboring communities. On Sunday, October 23, 1983, a truck loaded with over 2,000 pounds of explosives crashed through the barricades of the Marine compound and into the main military barracks. The ensuing explosion completely destroyed the building and tragically killed 241 American servicemen, the single largest loss of life of American military personnel since Vietnam. Simultaneously, the French military delegation was similarly bombed resulting in an additional 50 fatalities.

The vast majority of the young Marines were interred by family members in local cemeteries, but 21 of the bombing victims were brought to Arlington

National Cemetery to be buried in adjoining graves in Section 59. Subsequently, other victims of terrorism were interred in the same area, including First Lieutenant Dennis Keogh, who was killed in South Africa; Captain George Tsantes, assassinated in Greece; and CIA official Matthew Gannon, killed aboard Pan Am Flight 103 over Lockerbie, Scotland.

In 1984, the world's attention was riveted once again on the Middle East when two hijackers commandeered TWA Flight 847 en route from Athens to Rome. They held the plane's passengers and crew hostage for 17 days while crisscrossing the Mediterranean. After the plane had landed in Beirut for fuel, the terrorists callously murdered a Navy diver, SW2 Robert Stethem, and threw his body onto the tarmac. He was later interred in Section 59 near the other victims of terrorist violence. Each week, regardless of the weather or the time of year, Stethem's parents continue to decorate Robert's grave with fresh flowers, a silent reminder of the human toll of such insanity.

In 1984, No Greater Love, an organization originally founded to aid the children of soldiers missing or killed in action during the Vietnam War, organized a series of ceremonies to honor the Marines who had died in Lebanon as well as other victims of terrorist atrocities. On May 1, 1984, a 14-foot cedar of Lebanon was planted in Section 59 near the graves of the soldiers.

Congress approved a Joint Resolution to set aside the first anniversary of the Beirut bombing as "'A Time of Remembrance,' to urge all Americans to take time to reflect on the sacrifices that have been made in the pursuit of peace and freedom." On October 23, 1984, a memorial service was held at Arlington in Section 59 at which time a granite marker at the base of the cedar tree was unveiled. The inscription reads:

"Let Peace Take Root"
This Cedar of Lebanon tree grows in living memory
of the Americans killed in the Beirut terrorist attack
and all victims of terrorism throughout the world.
Dedicated during the first memorial ceremony for
these victims.

Given by No Greater Love   October 23, 1984
A Time of Remembrance

Section 59 has continued to serve as the primary burial location for American military personnel killed during terrorist assaults. However, this is an unofficial designation and other funerals routinely occur in the area.

CHAPTER NINE

Beyond the Stars

—Ronald Reagan

In May 1961, shortly after taking office, President John F. Kennedy responded to a series of dramatic Soviet space initiatives by announcing that the United States would undertake a massive effort to land a man on the moon by the end of the decade. In an address delivered before a joint session of Congress, President Kennedy stated: "No single space project in this period will be more impressive to mankind, or more important for the long-range exploration of space…in a very real sense, it will not be one man going to the moon…it will be an entire nation."

The National Aeronautics and Space Administration (N.A.S.A.) began a three-tier approach to achieving the President's goal. Beginning with six Mercury flights, the space program was scheduled to progress through a series of two-man Gemini launches and culminate with the lunar-capable Apollo missions.

The Mercury and Gemini flights proved to be stunning successes and a spirit of optimism surrounded the onset of the Apollo project. N.A.S.A. had assembled an impressive crew for the inaugural flight of *Apollo I*, consisting of three skilled and experienced astronauts: Virgil "Gus" Grissom, Edward White, and Roger "Bruce" Chaffee. Grissom was selected as the crew commander. He held the distinction of being the second American launched into space (July 21, 1961), just 11 weeks after the first Mercury mission by Alan Shepard. The 15-minute sub-orbital flight was marred, however, by the loss of Grissom's capsule, *Liberty Bell "7"*, which sank before recovery efforts could salvage it from the Atlantic. Despite this setback, Grissom served on the first Gemini flight in March 1965, thereby becoming the first American astronaut to serve on two space missions. Assisting Grissom on *Apollo I* was Astronaut Edward White. White had also served in the Gemini program and, in June 1965, became the first American to conduct a space-walk, leaving his capsule for a 20-minute tethered excursion into space. Roger Chaffee, a Navy test pilot, was the rookie of the mission with the flight of *Apollo I* to be his first venture into space.

Apollo I was scheduled for launch in late February 1967 and was to remain in earth orbit for up to 16 days. On January 27, just four weeks before the launch date, Grissom, Chaffee, and White entered their Apollo capsule for a series of preflight tests. Five hours into the mock countdown, the crew frantically radioed Mission Control that there was a fire on board the craft. Members of the attending launch-pad crew struggled to free the vessel's sealed hatch, a process which normally required a minimum of 90 seconds. Their heroic efforts, though, were hindered by the intense heat which was fueled by the capsule's pressurized oxygen. Six desperate minutes passed before the hatch finally sprung open and by that time all three astronauts were dead.

President Lyndon Johnson led the nation in mourning the loss of the nation's first space-related fatalities and attended separate funeral ceremonies at Arlington National Cemetery for Bruce Chaffee and Gus Grissom. The two astronauts were interred in adjoining graves in Section 3, appropriately near the grave of another aviation pioneer, Lieutenant Thomas Selfridge. The remains of astronaut Edward White were returned to New York for burial on the grounds of his alma mater, West Point.

Challenger

The Space Shuttle represented a new generation of spacecraft for the United States. Inaugurated on April 12, 1981 with the launch of *Columbia* (STS-1), the space vehicle and many of its component booster parts would be reusable. It was anticipated that an expanding fleet of shuttles would allow for 24 yearly launches and serve as an efficient transportation system for deploying satellites and ultimately component parts for an international space station. By 1986, just five years after its first flight, the shuttle program had been so successful that space travel appeared routine and the major television networks no longer offered live coverage of the launches.

The Space Shuttle *Challenger* was scheduled for its tenth launch on January 22, 1986. Mission 51-L was to last six days and was designed to deploy satellites for improved communications and for observation of Halley's Comet. It was particularly notable because it included the first private citizen ever to venture into space, teacher Christa McAuliffe, who had been selected from over 11,000 applicants for the "Teacher in Space" program. During the mission, she was to deliver a series of live lessons to the nation's school children in what she euphemistically called "the ultimate field trip."

Unseasonably cold temperatures repeatedly delayed the launch of the *Challenger*. Despite another frigid night, N.A.S.A. officials agreed to launch on January 28 after consultation with various shuttle contractors. Some 72 seconds into the flight at an altitude of 10 miles, the *Challenger* exploded after a failure of the critical O-ring seals on the solid rocket boosters which ignited the orbiter's massive external fuel tank. All seven crewmembers—Francis "Dick" Scobee, Michael Smith, Judith Resnick, Ellison Onizuka, Ronald McNair, Gregory Jarvis, and Christa McAuliffe—were killed, the first casual-

Astronauts White, Chaffee, and Grissom practice launch procedures aboard Apollo I. *A fire on board the capsule killed all three of the astronauts just four weeks before the scheduled launch.*

ties of the space program in 19 years.

Salvage and recovery efforts lasted several weeks while Navy and Coast Guard vessels combed the Atlantic seabed searching for debris. Identifiable remains of all the crewmembers were finally located and their bodies were returned to their families for burial some three months after their tragic deaths.

At his family's behest, Pilot Michael J. Smith was buried at Arlington

The flag-draped coffin of Astronaut Gus Grissom is escorted to the grave by fellow space pioneers John Glenn and Alan Shepard.

National Cemetery with full military honors in Section 7A, just below the Tomb of the Unknown Soldier and near the grave of heavyweight champion Joe Louis. His private monument bears air wings and a comet, the astronaut's insignia. Two weeks later, Mission Commander, Francis "Dick" Scobee was laid to rest on May 19, his forty-seventh birthday, in Section 46 adjacent to the grave of the three airmen who lost their lives during the Iranian hostage rescue mission. LTC Ellison Onizuka, U.S.A.F. was likewise buried with full military honors in Oahu, Hawaii at the Punch Bowl National Cemetery. The remains of the other astronauts were buried privately per their family's wishes. In an earlier memorial service at the Johnson Space Center honoring all of the *Challenger* crew, President Reagan eulogized: "The nation, too, will long feel the loss of her seven sons and daughters…we can find consolation only in faith, for we know in our hearts that you who flew so high and proud now make your home beyond the stars."

On the morning following the Scobee interment, representatives of all seven *Challenger* crewmembers quietly gathered in Section 46 prior to the normal scheduled opening of the cemetery. In a brief ceremony, an urn containing the ashes of the individually unidentifiable commingled remains of the crew that had been recovered from the crash site was placed and sealed into the concrete base of the anticipated *Challenger* memorial. At the request of the families, the service was conducted without publicity and no acknowledgment of the burial was allowed to be inscribed on the final memorial.

The following month, on June 10, 1986, Congress passed a concurrent resolution that stated, "It is the sense of Congress that the Secretary of the Army should construct and place at Arlington National Cemetery a memori-

U.S. Air Force Photo

Mrs. June Scobee places flowers on the grave of her husband, Space Shuttle Mission Commander Francis "Dick" Scobee. Michael Smith, the pilot of the ill-fated Challenger *was also buried at Arlington* al marker honoring the seven members of the crew of the Space shuttle *Challenger* who died on January 28, 1986 during the launch of the Space Shuttle Mission 51-L from Cape Canaveral." Although it was hoped that the monument would be ready for dedication on the first anniversary of the tragedy, the ceremony was delayed until March 21, 1987. At that time, Vice President George Bush unveiled and dedicated the granite monument which features a bronze plaque depicting the launch of the space shuttle surrounded by images of its seven crewmembers. On the back of the memorial is a quotation from the World War II-era poem, "High Flight," written by John Gillespie Magee, which was quoted by President Reagan during his speech to the nation concerning the fate of the *Challenger* crew.

Columbia

STS-107 was scheduled to be the last purely scientific mission of the space shuttle program due to the ever increasing demands for construction and maintenance of the new international space station. *Columbia* was the oldest of the four remaining shuttles and had successfully completed 27 space flights but the aging craft had never been designed to dock with the space station or equipped to carry related payloads. It was scheduled for a much needed overhaul after the completion of this mission.

The *Columbia's* flight crew consisted of seven astronauts—Cdr. Rick Husband, Pilot Willie McCool, Flight Engineer Kalpana "KC" Chawla, Payload Commander Michael Anderson, Payload Specialist Ilan Ramon, and Mission Specialists Dave Brown and Laurel Clark. Ramon, a highly decorated fighter pilot, had earned the distinction of becoming the first Israeli astronaut. His presence on the mission, however, led to concerns about possible terrorism and resulted in increased security measures.

On January 16, 2003 at 1039, the *Columbia* was launched successfully into low earth orbit. The take off was, from all outward appearances, routine but after analyzing film of the lift-off, NASA engineers became concerned about a previously undetected debris strike which had occurred during the initial stages of the launch. After several meetings and numerous emails, it was determined that a piece of insulating foam had detached from the external fuel tank and struck the orbiter's wing but that it was of such a composition and weight that it posed no significant risk either to the space craft or to the safety of the crew. Similar foam strikes had, in fact, occurred on earlier missions without significant damage or mishap and now had been deemed as an acceptable risk to fly. No effort was made by key N.A.S.A. officials to utilize military spy satellites to photograph the shuttle in orbit to verify these conclusions. In reality, the briefcase-size piece of insulating foam, although weighing less than two pounds, had slammed into the orbiter's wing at over 500 miles per hour and the impact caused massive damage to several of the wing's crucial reinforced carbon-carbon (R.C.C.) tiles. The resulting 9-inch hole made a safe re-entry impossible and had effectively doomed the crew.

The *Columbia's* astronauts could not see the damage to the wing from their space craft and were unaware of the impending disaster. They continued with their scientific experiments and other duties pausing briefly on January 28, the seventeenth anniversary of the *Challenger* explosion, to honor their lost comrades. Commander Rick Husband radioed from space, "It is today that we remember and honor the crews of *Apollo I* and *Challenger*. They made the ultimate sacrifice, giving their lives and service to their country and for all mankind. Their dedication and devotion to the exploration of space was an inspiration to each of us and still motivates people around the world to achieve great things and service to others." At that time, ten American astronauts and four Soviet cosmonauts had been killed as a direct result of manned-space flight.

On the morning of February 1 as scheduled, *Columbia* began its initial descent from orbit. Reentering the earth's atmosphere at 18 times the speed of sound, the gapping hole in the left wing soon allowed white hot gasses to penetrate the shuttle's internal structural elements and led to a catastrophic break up of the craft. The orbiter and its entire crew were lost at 08:59:32 at an altitude of 207,135 feet. The resulting debris field extended over a 12,500 square mile area of Texas and Louisiana.

Later that afternoon, President George W. Bush formally addressed the nation: "My fellow Americans, this day has brought terrible news and great sadness to our country. At 9 o'clock this morning, Mission Control in Houston lost contact with our space shuttle *Columbia*. A short time later, debris was seen falling from the skies about Texas. The *Columbia* is lost; there are no survivors...Mankind is led into the darkness beyond our world by the inspiration of discovery and the longing to understand...The same Creator who names the stars also knows the names of the seven souls we mourn today. The crew of the shuttle *Columbia* did not return safely to Earth; yet we can pray that all are safely home. May God bless the grieving families, and may God continue to bless America."

Recovery efforts began immediately and ultimately 84,900 pieces of the shuttle would be salvaged. Just two days after the accident, it was announced that the remains of all seven astronauts had been found, all within close proximity to one another. The bodies were sent to Dover Air Force base for final identification. Using DNA analysis, dental records, x-rays, and other forensic techniques, all of the remains were quickly identified and returned to their individual families for burial. Ramon's body was flown back to Israel where he was interred on February 11, according to Jewish law and custom, while Chawla's ashes were buried in her native India. Funeral services for Cdr. Husband and Pilot McCool were conducted in their native states of Texas and Washington while the remaining three astronauts were buried at Arlington National Cemetery with full military honors. (The first of the Arlington funerals took place on Friday, March 7).

The crew of the Space Shuttle Columbia *shortly before launch on January 16, 2001. The shuttle broke up upon reentry killing the entire crew.*

NASA

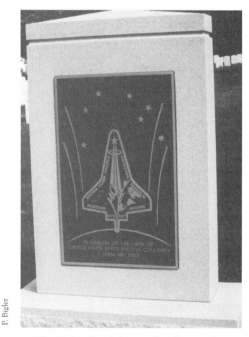

P. Bigler

The Columbia *Memorial in Section 46. Three of the astronauts were interred at Arlington Cemetery*

Air Force Lt. Colonel Michael Anderson was buried in Section 46 near the grave of Challenger Commander Dick Scobee. In honor of Col. Anderson's previous military service with the 389 Refueling Wing, a KC-135 Stratotanker with its refueling boom fully extended flew over the gravesite in final tribute. Chaplain Richard Hum noted that "It is here [at Arlington] that for nearly 150 years America has chosen to place their heroes." The following Monday on what would have been her forty-second birthday, Astronaut Laurel Clark (Capt.-USN) was laid to rest next to her friend and crewmate. A Scottish bag-piper played "Scotland the Brave." Clark, a Navy flight surgeon and novice in space, was survived by her husband, Jon, and their young son, Ian. On March 12, the last of the seven Columbia crew, Captain David Brown (USN), was buried at Arlington. He had grown up in the Washington, D.C., area and attended the local Yorktown High School before commissioning and becoming a pilot and a doctor. During his funeral service, four F-18 fighter jets flew over the cemetery in the missing man formation. A close friend of Brown's, Captain Gordon Iiams (USN-Ret), appropriately remarked "All seven of those folks on that space craft, that shuttle, were wonderful people. They were all like Dave."

One year and a day after the loss of the Columbia, a memorial to the crew was unveiled during private ceremonies at Arlington National Cemetery. Virtually identical in size and shape to that of the adjacent

Challenger monument, the gray granite marker features a bronze tablet engraved with the STS-107 mission patch with 7 stars representing each of the fallen astronauts. It is inscribed:

In Memory of the Crew of
United States Space Shuttle Columbia
1 February 2003

On the reverse in low relief, is a depiction of the crew as they were photographed prior to launch. The intimate ceremony was closed to the public but was broadcast live over NASA television with Administrator Sean O'Keefe presiding. He eulogized:

> Today we remember and commemorate the undaunted courage of seven true heroes for our time, and for all times, our Columbia STS-107 astronauts…Arlington National Cemetery also provides a final resting place for great heroes who changed the course of history by blazing new trails of exploration and discovery…The hallowed ground of Arlington National Cemetery honors many NASA astronauts who took up the President's call to lead our way into the new frontier of space, including members of the Apollo One, Challenger and Columbia crews . . . Generations from now, when the reach of human civilization is extended throughout the solar system, people will still come to this place to learn about and pay their respects to our heroic Columbia astronauts. They will look at the astronauts' memorial and then they will turn their gaze to the skies, their hearts filled with gratitude for these seven brave explorers who helped blaze our trail to the stars.

The anniversaries of all three of the nation's space tragedies fall within a week of one another: *Apollo I* – January 27; *Challenger* – January 28; and *Columbia* – February 1.

The Persian Gulf War

On August 2, 1990, the world was stunned when Iraq launched a massive military invasion of neighboring Kuwait. The small, oil-rich Persian Gulf kingdom was quickly overrun and Saddam Hussein proclaimed it to be Iraq's nineteenth province.

President George H.W. Bush countered by declaring that such naked aggression would not be tolerated and began to assemble a diverse and powerful military coalition to oppose Hussein. The President immediately ordered American military forces to the region, initiating the largest deployment of the United States armed services since the Vietnam War. By mid-January, some 514,000 American servicemen and women had been assembled and were in position in Saudi Arabia.

Despite numerous pronouncements and ultimatums by the United Nations, Hussein steadfastly refused to withdraw from Kuwait. On January 16, 1991, President Bush ordered coalition forces into action. *Operation Desert Storm* began with a massive air offensive against Baghdad and other Iraqi military targets.

With American military forces fully engaged in combat, Arlington and the nations other national cemeteries were ordered to stand by to receive potential casualties but the air war proved exceptionally efficient and coalition losses remained remarkably light. Still, on February 15, Arlington received its first casualty from the conflict, Captain Jonathan Edwards, who was killed in action when his AH-1 Cobra helicopter crashed near the Kuwaiti border. That same day, a memorial stone was erected for 1LT Jorge Arteaga whose body was not recovered after his B-52 crashed into the Indian Ocean, apparently shot down by Iraqi defenses.

Because of the scope of the American military commitment, President Bush had called up over 40,000 reservists to active duty. Most of these troops were utilized in support positions to assist with maintenance, logistics, and supply. The 476th Quartermaster Corps from Greensburg, Pennsylvania, was a military police detachment that had been assigned to duty in Dhahran, Saudi Arabia. On February 25, as the soldiers were finishing dinner, an Iraqi SCUD missile slammed into their barracks, killing 27 and wounding over 100 others. While most of the casualties were buried in Pennsylvania near the unit's headquarters, PFC Timothy Shaw was buried with military honors at Arlington Cemetery in Section 8.

The Persian Gulf War officially ended on February 28 with the liberation of Kuwait and the surrender of thousands of Iraqi troops. Still, despite the cease-fire, the military continued to conduct dangerous mine sweeping operations, air patrols, and humanitarian missions. On March 1, 32-year-old Major Marie Rossi volunteered to fly a mission despite the onset of bad weather. Rossi had gained distinction during the war for her bravery and for having flown into combat. In many ways, she had become a symbol of the ever-expanding role of women in the United States military. On this mission, however, her Chinook helicopter crashed, killing Major Rossi and her crew. She was buried in a grave adjacent to that of PFC Shaw. Her family eulogized, "We are proud as we can be of [Marie's] accomplishments in the service of her country; and we are proud of her bravery, her leadership and her example to others." On Major Rossi's headstone is inscribed, "First Female Combat Commander to Fly in Battle." On the reverse of the monument is a bronze plaque featuring a Chinook helicopter and the fitting sentiment "May our men and women stand strong and equal."

Eventually, 17 casualties from the Persian Gulf War were buried at Arlington. In addition, nine memorial stones were erected in honor of servicemen who lost their lives and whose remains were unrecoverable.

U.S. Navy Photo

*The remains of the barracks of the 476th Quartermaster Corps after it was struck by
an Iraqi SCUD missile near the end of the Persian Gulf Conflict. PFC Timothy Shaw
was among the 27 killed in the attack and was buried with military
honors at Arlington Cemetery.*

September 11, 2001

September 11 was a beautiful, cloudless late summer day in the Washington, D.C., area. At Arlington, it began routinely with a full day of funerals scheduled and Superintendent Jack Metzler preparing to go to Capitol Hill where he was due to testify on proposed legislation for land acquisition and cemetery expansion.

At 0845 hours, American Airlines Flight 11 slammed into the north tower of the World Trade Center in New York City. As news of the disaster quickly spread, a television was commandeered at Arlington's main administration building for cemetery personnel to watch portions of the unfolding story while continuing to work. Most logically assumed that the horrific crash had been a tragic accident but these delusions were shattered when another plane crashed into the adjacent south tower just 18 minutes later revealing far more sinister motives. It was now obvious that the United States was under an unprecedented terrorist attack.

At 0937 another plane—American Airlines Flight 77—flew directly over the Navy Annex and the southern portions of the cemetery targeted for the Pentagon. It hit the building's newly reinforced concrete western wall at an estimated 460 miles per hour. The resulting cataclysmic explosion caused by the high-speed impact and burning jet fuel shook buildings and rattled windows throughout Arlington and nearby Crystal City. Superintendent Jack Metzler responded at once by ordering that the cemetery be shut down to tourists and visitors as the nation's entire military command structure rapidly shifted into its highest state of alert.

Rescue and recovery operations at the Pentagon began immediately with area police and firefighters responding to the crash site, augmenting military personnel already on the scene. Members of the 3d United States Infantry, The Old Guard, from Fort Myer were dispatched to assist with the rescue efforts and a temporary triage area and helipad were set up to airlift the injured to local area hospitals. Other honor guard troops scheduled for funeral detail were withdrawn for force protection. Simultaneously, the Pentagon was partially evacuated with some of the survivors taking refuge within the nearby boundaries of the cemetery.

As the scope of the tragedy was becoming more apparent, Arlington still had several funerals scheduled. Cemetery representatives informed family members who had already arrived at the main administration building of all that had transpired and gave them the option of postponing their services to a later date. Many, however, chose to proceed rather than prolong an already painful grieving process. Indeed, at 1000 hours, just minutes after the crash, a graveside service with military body bearers was conducted for the spouse of a veteran and was completed with all of the prerequisite dignity and honor despite the plainly visible dark, black smoke billowing up into the morning sky from the nearby crash site and the presence of helicopters hovering overhead. Yet even with the developing events and the eventual withdrawal of military support, several other funerals were completed at Arlington throughout the rest of the day.

At 1010 hours, a large portion of the Pentagon's E-Ring outer wall collapsed as the intense fires from the highly volatile jet fuel continued to rage. Despite the building's extensive damage, Secretary of Defense, Donald Rumsfeld, and Chairman of the Joint Chiefs of Staff, Army Gen. Henry Shelton, reassured the American public that the Pentagon would remain operational and functioning while the United States military was prepared to respond to any further acts of aggression. F-14 jet fighters were now on combat air patrol over the nation's capital while all civilian aircraft throughout the nation had been grounded by orders from the Federal Aviation Administration.

The following day with the Pentagon ruins still smoldering, President George W. Bush visited the crash site to view the devastation caused by the impact of the huge American Airlines Boeing 757. In a speech given to recovery workers, the President stated, "Coming here makes me sad, on the one

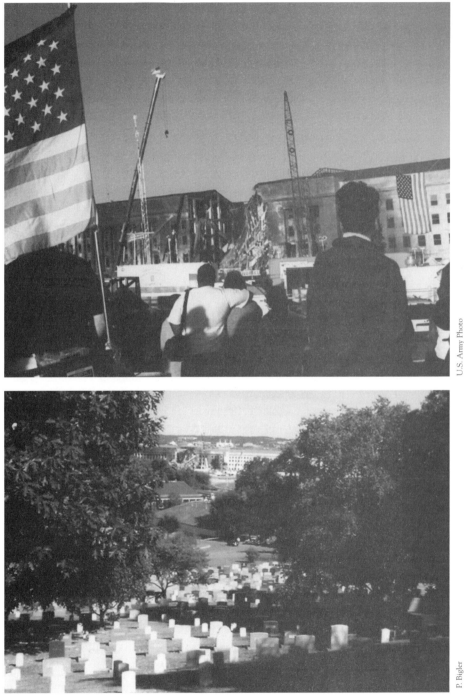

U.S. Army Photo

P. Bigler

The Pentagon viewed from Arlington Cemetery shortly after the 9-11 terrorist attacks.
American Airlines Flight 77 was hijacked from Dulles International Airport and flew
directly over the cemetery before striking the Pentagon

hand; it also makes me angry. Our country will, however, not be cowed by terrorists, by people who don't share the same values we share, by people who are
willing to destroy people's lives because we embrace freedom. The nation
mourns, but our government will go on, the country will function. We are on
high alert for possible activity." An enormous garrison flag sent to the site
from Fort Myer by the U.S. Army Band was unfurled over the side of the
building by firefighters and military personal to serve as a powerful symbol of
the nation's resolve.

Arlington, likewise, represented the country's patriotic spirit by reopen-
ing to visitation on Saturday, September 15 although with a substantial
increase in security. Park police officers restricted public access to the sections
closest to the Pentagon so that recovery operations were not hindered.
Funerals, however, had continued throughout the week although many were
temporarily postponed at the behest of some families because of the closure of
Washington's Ronald Reagan National Airport and the public's general reluctance to fly in the aftermath of the terrorist hijackings.

Over the next several weeks, officials at the Pentagon issued regular
updates concerning casualty figures. Recovered remains were sent to Dover
Air Force Base for positive identification before being finally released to family members. Within two weeks of the attack, the first burials of the Pentagon
victims began at Arlington. Among these were Navy Commander Patrick
Dunn and Lt. Cdr Otis Tobert who were interred in Section 64 just a few hundred yards from the crash site. Three of the 59 victims aboard American
Airlines Flight 77 were interred at the cemetery including the plane's captain,
Navy reservist, Charles "Chic" Burlingame. Ultimately, 64 of the casualties
would be buried at Arlington National Cemetery.

Memorial Gravesite

Over the next year, construction workers labored around the clock to repair
the gaping hole in the Pentagon. Known as *Operation Phoenix*, the $700 mil-
lion restoration was completed with remarkable speed, under budget, and in
time for the nationwide one-year commemorations of the September 11
attacks. President George W. Bush, accompanied by the First Lady and the
Secretary of Defense, participated in the "United in Freedom" ceremony conducted in front of the Pentagon's newly restored façade. A moment of silence
was observed at precisely 0937, the official time of impact of AA Flight 77.

The next day, September 12, Secretary Rumsfeld presided over the final
funeral service for victims of the Pentagon attack at Arlington's Memorial
Amphitheater, the first such observance at the building since the burial of the
Vietnam Unknown in 1984. Partial, commingled remains of 25 victims were
consigned to a single casket for group burial in Section 64. A special place of
honor was reserved for the families of the five victims whose bodies had never
been identified or recovered. Four had worked for the Department of Defense

The Pentagon Memorial in Section 64. The five-sided monument lists the name of all 184 victims of the terrorist attack against the Pentagon on September 11, 2001.

at the Pentagon: Col. Ronald Golinski (USA-ret.), Navy Petty Officer 1st Class Ronald Hemenway, Rhonda Rasmussen, and James Lynch. The fifth was 3-year-old Dana Falkenberg, a passenger on board Flight 77, who had been en route to Australia with her parents and sister when the plane was hijacked. Extraordinary care and extensive DNA testing ensured that all traces of the remains of the terrorists had been isolated, separated and removed to prevent any desecration of Arlington's soil.

The invocation at the Amphitheater was delivered by BG David Hicks and was followed by the hymn, "O God Our Help in Ages Past," and readings from the New and Old Testaments. BG James T. Spivey delivering the funeral address before Secretary of Defense Donald Rumsfeld formally offered the nation's condolences:

> Those we honor today died here at home—not on a faraway battlefield. They died within view of this cemetery. Yet they did die on a battlefield—and that battlefield tells us a great deal about the war we are in—the first war of the 21st Century...
>
> When this ceremony is over, you may look again at the memorial, note the names that are special to you, take a final moment—have a last word, or look, or prayer. Then turn and leave this place, feeling again the emptiness, thinking again of the 'tomorrow and tomorrow and tomorrow' of an irreplaceable,

seemingly endless loss.

And you might say again, what so many times this year you may have said to yourselves...that we can be grateful for the time we had with them, that we must trust in a loving God who holds them close and affords them now the greatest of peace and joy...

And so, today, we honor the 184 patriots who died at the Pentagon last September 11. We remember, with special love, the five whose remains were not recovered, and their families and friends who were denied the peace that comes with placing loved ones in their final place of take a break.

This day these five join the unknown of wars past, even as we pursue the war that is still unfolding. Known and unknown, those resting here were bound in brotherhood by their heritage. Soldier and civilian alike, they were dedicated to the cause of freedom. They will be remembered. We will not forget.

At the conclusion of the memorial services, the casket was placed upon a horse-drawn caisson and transported to Section 64 for committal. At the gravesite was a pentagon-shaped wreath consisting of 184 flowers representing each of the September 11 deceased including five white flowers to symbolize the unidentified. Nearby, were the rows of graves of 57 (seven others had been interred elsewhere in the cemetery) of their compatriots, each marked by an identical white government headstone. The bronze-colored crypt cover bore the Department of Defense seal and was inscribed, "Victims of Terrorist Attack on the Pentagon, September 11, 2001." A special, pentagon shaped monument, inscribed on five sides with all of the names of the 125 Pentagon workers and 59 AA-77 passengers and crew who lost their lives on September 11, 2001, will forever mark the memorial grave which stands in silent testament near the site of the horrific attack.

The War on Terror

On October 7, 2001, just 26 days after the devastating September 11 attacks against the United States, the Bush administration launched *Operation Enduring Freedom* against the Taliban in Afghanistan. The radical Islamic government had continued to provide comfort and sanctuary to Osama bin Laden and his al-Qaeda terrorist network despite international pressure and global condemnation.

Aided by the nationalist Afghan Northern Alliance and a coalition of military forces, the operations were successful in disrupting the entire terrorist infrastructure. Captured documents and videotapes uncovered elaborate plans for future terrorist attacks against American facilities and nuclear reactors as well as chronicling a frightening effort to develop and obtain an arsenal chemical, biological, and nuclear weapons.

U.S. Army Photo

A car bombing in downtown Baghdad. Despite an impressive and rapid military victory over Iraqi forces, terrorists continued to plague the US-led occupation of Iraq.

On November 25, 2001, Michael Spann became the first American combat casualty of the Afghan war. He was killed while interrogating prisoners near Mazar-i-Sharif. A former Marine, Spann had joined the CIA in 1999 and was serving with the agency's Special Activities Division. He was buried with full military honors at Arlington National Cemetery in Section 34. During the funeral ceremonies, his wife, Shannon, honored her husband's memory: "[he] is a hero, but Mike is a hero not because of the way that he died but rather because of the way that he lived. Mike was prepared to give his life in Afghanistan because he already gave his life every day to us at home." CIA Director George Tenet likewise eulogized that Spann had gone to Afghanistan "in the quest for right...to bring justice and freedom."

Although the Taliban government quickly collapsed, bin Laden avoided capture by seeking safe haven in the rugged, mountainous regions near the eastern Afghan border. With the cooperation and assistance of the Pakistani government, Special Operations continued the search for the elusive al-Qaeda leader. By the summer of 2004, American casualties in ongoing operations in Afghanistan had reached 119.

With the initial successes in Afghanistan, the focus of America's continuing war on terrorism shifted to Iraq. Although he lost the Persian Gulf War a decade earlier, Saddam Hussein remained firmly entrenched in power and was suspected by the international community of stockpiling both chemical and biological weapons, so-called weapons of mass destruction (W.M.D.). During his January 2002 State of the Union address, President Bush denounced Iraq as part of an "Axis of Evil" in the world:

> Iraq continues to flaunt its hostility toward America and to support terror. The Iraqi regime has plotted to develop anthrax, and nerve gas, and nuclear weapons for over a decade. This is a regime that has already used poison gas to murder thousands of its own citizens—leaving the bodies of mothers huddled over their dead children. This is a regime that agreed to international inspections—then kicked out the inspectors. This is a regime that has something to hide from the civilized world.

Support for further combat action, however, was limited and outwardly opposed by the French, Germans, and Russians. With a threatened veto in the Security Council of any resolution authorizing military force, the United States and Great Britain chose to act unilaterally. On March 17, 2004, President George W. Bush issued a formal ultimatum to the Iraqi dictator: "Saddam Hussein and his sons must leave Iraq within 48 hours. Their refusal to go will result in military conflict commenced at a time of our choosing."

Two days later, *Operation Iraqi Freedom* began with the launch of dozens of cruise missiles against Saddam Hussein's Baghdad headquarters in an effort to kill the Iraqi leader in what was termed a "decapitation" strike. Although unsuccessful, U.S. airpower conducted an impressive "shock and awe" campaign designed to demoralize the Iraqi military and lessen military resistance by an overwhelming show of force. In a simultaneous land campaign, allied British and American forces crossed the Iraqi border from bases in Kuwait. By March 22, the US 3rd Infantry Division had progressed 150 miles, half the distance to the Iraqi capital while the British were in the process of securing the crucial city of Basra.

The march to Baghdad was rapid but perilous and not without casualties. The first soldier from the campaign to be buried at Arlington was 27-year-old Army Captain Russell B. Rippetoe, 3rd Battalion, 75th Ranger Company. He was killed on April 3 when a car bomb exploded at a military checkpoint near the Hadithah Dam. Within a week of his interment, six more soldiers had been buried at Arlington, most in Section 60.

By March 28, U.S. forces had reached the outskirts of Baghdad with troops on high alert for a potential chemical attack. Within a few days, American troops were making regular incursions into the capital as formal military resistance crumbled. On April 9, the imposing statue of Saddam Hussein was toppled in Firdos Square, symbolically ending his brutal dictatorship. On May 1, President George Bush landed on the aircraft carrier, U.S.S. *Abraham Lincoln,* and declared an end to the combat phase of the war in which the United States had sustained less than 150 combat casualties

GI Cartoonist Bill Mauldin was buried at Arlington in 2003. The passing of the World War II generation increased demands for burial space and served as a catalyst for Arlington's much needed expansion.

Emerging from decades of totalitarian rule and making the transition to democracy in Iraq, however, proved difficult as rival factions and radical groups struggled for power. Attacks against American and British forces with rocket-propelled grenades, roadside bombs, and suicide bombers became a daily occurrence and by the end of the year, casualties approached 500 with 45 of those soldiers buried at Arlington. In April 2004, 136 Americans lost their lives in Iraq, the bloodiest month to date since Arlington began receiving active duty deaths from the conflict.

The Greatest Generation

With the advent of the new century, Congress, the Department of Defense, and the Veterans Administration (V.A.) began serious discussions concerning the much-needed expansion of Arlington. With the cemetery using approximately 2,200 new graves annually (two-thirds of Arlington's 6,000 burials were in existing family plots), it became clear that Arlington was rapidly approaching its capacity at the same time that the need for grave space in national cemeteries was reaching its peak.

Over 16 million Americans had patriotically answered their nation's call during World War II and served honorably in the country's armed services. The United States census indicated that 4.7 million veterans were still living in the year 2000, but it noted that the "Greatest Generation" was a rapidly aging population with a median age of 78. It was estimated that 1,100 veterans died each day. The government predicted that demand for grave space in America's national cemeteries would peak in 2008 when, in that year alone, over 620,000 World War II era servicemen and women were expected to pass away, triple the total number of American combat casualties during the entire war. Each veteran had earned suitable military honors, appropriate burial space, and the nation's gratitude.

The V.A. was determined to accommodate all eligible veterans and began the planning, development, and construction of several new cemeteries. In November 2001, the Fort Sill National Cemetery in Oklahoma began operations with 391 acres and 166,000 available graves. Eleven additional sites have been authorized by Congress to be opened in Alabama, California (2), Florida (3), Georgia, Michigan, Pennsylvania (2), and South Carolina.

Congress likewise began to consider Arlington's desperate need for additional acreage. In 1999, President Bill Clinton signed into law the FY2000 Defense Authorizations Act, which sanctioned the cemetery's eventual annexation of land from adjacent military bases. The Navy Annex, initially constructed during World War II, was scheduled to be demolished within 15 years, thereby opening its 37 acres to burial, although some lawmakers favored designating three of its acres for the construction of an Air Force Memorial.

In addition, Fort Myer would cede an additional eight acres of land to the cemetery. These future acquisitions were anticipated to provide roughly 30,000 graves, thereby ensuring Arlington's ongoing operation until at least 2060. To meet Arlington's immediate land needs, the National Park Service returned 12 acres of wooded land near the Lee Mansion. The acquisition increased the cemetery's size to its current 624 acres.

The Columbarium

Many American veterans, despite their honorable and distinguished service, were no longer allowed to be buried at Arlington National Cemetery because of the extensive grave conservation effort and increasingly rigorous eligibility requirements. Yet many of these servicemen still desired interment at the cemetery. The Department of the Army in conjunction with the Veterans Administration began to investigate various alternatives to in-ground burial in an effort to accommodate all honorably discharged veterans. Mr. Raymond Costanzo, the superintendent of Arlington, became a leading advocate for the construction of a columbarium for cremated remains: "The change in the eligibility criteria in the late 60s was very unpopular. There were thousands of veterans that wanted to be buried [at Arlington] and since the new regulations did not permit it, we came up with this concept – the columbarium – whereby cremated remains of veterans could be placed here."

The first structure was formally dedicated in 1980 with another complet-

P. Bigler

The Columbarium for cremated remains opened in 1980. Eventually nine such structures are planned.

ed in 1985. To date, seven courts have been completed with two more additions planned, which will ultimately provide a total of 50,000 niches capable of accommodating 100,000 remains. The columbarium has proven to be a successful and popular addition to the cemetery. "We anticipated about 700 [inurnments] per year," Costanzo recalled, "It's running well over 1,000 per year and growing steadily. It's something I think is good for the veterans."

The Women in Military Service Memorial

The Arlington Memorial Archway was originally intended to provide a grand entrance into the cemetery. Commissioned during the Great Depression, the structure was never completely finished and failed to achieve its intended purpose.

In the mid-1980's General Wilma Vaught (USAF-ret) and members of the Women in Military Service for America Foundation, secured permission from the National Capitol Memorial Commission to use the archway as part of a monument to honor the 1.8 million women who had served in the Armed Services. A design competition was held, and in November 1989, the project was awarded to architects Marion Weiss and Michael Manfredi.

The initial design incorporated an innovative use of skylights, prisms, and glass spires that would provide a soft glow at night. The National Capitol Memorial Commission, however, feared that such a design was incompatible with the Kennedy gravesite and required substantial modifications to ensure

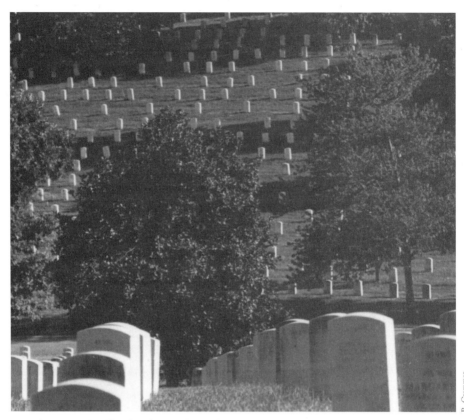

R. Crammer

The rows of endless headstones bear silent testimony to the nation's military heroes.

the integrity of the eternal flame.

After the final plans were approved, construction of the new memorial began on June 22, 1995. The finished monument was formally dedicated during a four-day celebration in October 1997. The Women in Military Service Memorial houses a theater, an exhibit area, and a computerized register of women veterans. It serves to recognize the contributions and honorable service that women have historically provided to the United States both in peacetime and at war.

The Future of Arlington

Despite Arlington's increasing number of visitors, for almost 20 years two small trailers served as the cemetery's only visitor's center. Although these structures were intended to be temporary, government budget constraints prevented the replacement of the inadequate facilities until 1986 when ground was finally broken for a new $8 million complex. The new building was formally opened in 1988 and now provides tourist and visitors to the cemetery an appropriate orientation to Arlington. The building features an impressive display of mural-size photographs documenting many of the important events in the cemetery's history along with a grave information counter and a bookstore. Display cases are located throughout the building with rotating exhibits. Tickets are likewise available for tourist transportation throughout the cemetery grounds. Former Superintendent Raymond Costanzo was a determined advocate for the creation of a new Visitors Center for the cemetery and believes that the building is "...a place where the visitors can be well received in a quality atmosphere." Furthermore, he feels that tourist will be able to "...get a brief orientation of what the cemetery's all about and then visually enjoy it."

In December 1990, Costanzo retired after 18 years of distinguished service. On January 14, 1991, in the midst of the Persian Gulf conflict, John C. Metzler assumed the superintendent's duties. Metzler, the son of a former Arlington chief, had grown up on the cemetery's grounds and had witnessed many of its most historic moments, including the funerals of John and Robert Kennedy. During the Vietnam War, he served as a helicopter crew chief and later became the director of several national cemeteries. Under his current leadership, Arlington continued to serve the nation by honoring its veterans during both times of war and peace.

Arlington completed its 230,000th burial in 1993. In April 2002, the cemetery exhausted its supply of graves in private monument sections, but with the anticipated expansion of the columbarium coupled with the new land acquisitions, Arlington's future as an active military cemetery is secure for at least another 60 years. After that time, it will be maintained as a national shrine.

Periodically, the world's attention will again focus on Arlington National Cemetery as the nation's burial ground. The greatest future for Arlington, though, was envisioned by President John F. Kennedy when he foresaw a time when "...there will be no veterans of any further wars...because all shall have learned to live together in peace." When that time comes, perhaps those who will continue to be buried at Arlington will be remembered not for how they died, but for the contributions they made while living. Meanwhile, the countless headstones at Arlington National Cemetery serve as a silent reminder of the valor of those American servicemen and women who eternally rest...*in honored glory.*

APPENDIX A
NOTABLE NAMES AND BURIAL LOCATIONS

NAME	SEC.	GRAVE
Anderson, Michael Columbia Astronaut	46	1180-1
Arnold, Henry Gen. Of the Army	34	44-A
Batista, Marlo Italian POW	15C	347-A
Berger, Warren Chief Justice	5	7015-2
Boyington, Pappy Col.	7A	176
Bradley, Omar Gen. Of the Army	30	428-1&2
Brown, David Columbia Astronaut	46	1180-3
Brown, Ron Sec. Of commerce	6	8389-B
Bryan, William Jennings	4	3118
Burlingame, Charles Pilot, AA 77	35	4288
Chaffee, Roger Bruce Apollo I Astronaut	3	2502-F
Chennault, Clair Lt. Gen.	2	873-4
Christman, William Henry Pvt.	27	19
Clark, Laurel, Columbia Astronaut	46	1180-2
Commerford, John Superintendent	1	545-WS
Clifford, Clark Sec. of Defense	7A	35
Conrad, Pete Apollo XII Astronaut	7A	
Costanzo, Raymond Superintendent	7A	191
Davis, Benjamin O. Gen. Tuskegee Airmen	6-M4	15-5
Doolittle, Jimmy Gen.	7A	111
Doubleday, Abner Gen.	1	61
Dulles, John Foster Sec. Of State	21	S-31
Evers, Medgar Civil Rights Advocate	36	1431
Gagnon, Rene Cpl.	51	543
Grissom, Virgil Apollo I Astronaut	3	2503-F
Halsey, William Fleet Admiral	2	1184
Hayes, Ira Cpl.	34	479-A
Henson, Matthew Arctic Explorer	8	LOT S-15
Hilberath, Anton German POW	15C	347-1
Holmes, Oliver Wendell Justice	5	LOT 7004-A
Hopper, Grace Murray Rear Admiral	59	973
Irwin, James Apollo XV Astronaut	3	2503-G-2
Kearny, Philip Gen.	2	LOT S-8
L'Enfant, Pierre	2	LOT 3
Lansdowne, Zachary LCDR	4	3122
Leahy, William Fleet Admiral	2	932
Lincoln, Robert Todd	31	LOT 13
Lingan, James McCubbin Gen.	1	LOT 299
Louis, Joe Heavyweight Champion	7A	177
MacArthur, Arthur Gen.	2	879
Marshall, George C. Gen. of the Army	7	LOT 8198
Marshall, Thurgood Justice	5	40-3
Marvin, Lee Actor	7A	176
Mauldin, Bill Sgt. GI Cartoonist	64	6974
McAuliffe, Anthony Gen.	3	2536
Meigs, Montgomery Gen.	1	LOT 1
Metzler, John J. Superintendent	7A	86
Miller, Glen GI Band Leader	MH	464-A
Mitchell, John Attorney General	7A	121
Moynihan, Daniel Patrick Senator	36	2261

APPENDIX B
ARLINGTON CHRONOLOGY

1608   Captain John Smith explores the upper Potomac River in the vicinity of Arlington.

1669   Robert Howsing receives a six thousand acre land grant from Governor Berkeley of Virginia.

1778   John Parke Custis, the son of Martha Washington, purchases the eleven hundred acre Arlington tract.

1781   After the Battle of Yorktown, John Parke Custis dies from illness.

1802   The construction of Arlington House begins.

1803   George Washington Parke Custis marries Mary Lee Fitzhugh.

1824   The Marquis de Lafayette visits the Arlington estate while on a grand tour of the United States.

1831   Mary Custis weds Robert E. Lee at Arlington House.

1857   George Washington Parke Custis dies and entails the land to his daughter, Mary Custis Lee.

1861   Robert E. Lee leaves Arlington to join the Virginia state militia; Union troops cross the Potomac and occupy the estate.

1862   Congress passes "An Act for the Collection of Taxes in Insurrectionary Districts."

1864   William H. Christman and William H. McKinney are the first soldiers buried on the Arlington estate; the cemetery is formally commissioned.

1866   2,111 unknowns are buried in a crypt near the Arlington mansion.

1868   General Logan issues Order #11 creating "Decoration Day."

1870   Robert E. Lee dies in Lexington, Virginia.

1872   Regulations require the use of uniform stones in enlisted areas.

1873   Mary Custis Lee visits her old Arlington home; she dies five months later and is buried along side her husband in Lexington, Virginia.

1874   The "old" Amphitheater is dedicated near the Arlington House mansion.

1882   The United States Supreme Court declares the federal government a trespasser and orders the estate returned to its antebellum condition.

1883   Custis Lee sells Arlington to the federal government for $150,000.

1888   Memorial Day is declared a national holiday.

1889   Arlington annexes 142 acres of land.

1892   The first Revolutionary War dead are reinterred to Arlington.

1897   Arlington annexes 56 acres of land.

1899   The first Spanish-American War casualties are buried in the cemetery, the first time that American soldiers are returned from foreign soil for interment.

1902   The Spanish-American War Memorial is dedicated.

1903   Arlington burials reach 19,000; 300 funerals are being conducted annually.

1905   Fourteen Unknowns from the War of 1812 are buried in Section 1.

1908   Lt. Thomas Selfridge, the first casualty of powered flight, is buried at Arlington after the crash of a plane piloted by Orville Wright.

1909   Pierre L'Enfant, the designer of the city of Washington, D.C., is buried in front of Arlington House on a ridge overlooking the nation's capital.

1915   Construction of the Memorial Amphitheater begins; Woodrow Wilson lays the corner stone.

1920   The Memorial Amphitheater is dedicated.

1921   The World War I Unknown Soldier is buried on the plaza of the Amphitheater.

1925   Restoration of the Arlington House mansion is begun.

1926   Robert Todd Lincoln, the son of President Abraham Lincoln, is interred at Arlington Cemetery on a hill overlooking the Lincoln Memorial.

1930   Former President and Chief Justice of the Supreme Court, William Howard Taft, becomes the first chief executive buried at Arlington.

1932   The capstone to the Tomb of the Unknown Soldier is completed, bringing the Tomb to its present shape; the Memorial Bridge connecting Arlington to Washington, D.C. is completed.

1933   Arlington House is transferred to the jurisdiction of the National Park Service.

1937   The Tomb of the Unknown Soldier is placed under a twenty-four hour honor guard; the Memorial Gateway is dedicated providing the western terminus to Memorial Bridge.

1940   At year's end, 49,927 Americans have been buried at Arlington Cemetery.

1941   Ignace Paderewski is allowed temporary repose in the Mast of the U.S.S. *Maine* Memorial.

1944   Manuel Quezon of the Philippines also is allowed temporary repose in the Mast of the U.S.S. *Maine* Memorial until his nation is liberated from the Japanese.

1945   The first World War II prisoners of war are buried at Arlington in accordance with the Geneva Convention.

1948   General of the Armies John J. "Black Jack" Pershing, the former commander of the American Expeditionary Forces, is buried; President Truman issues Executive Order 9981 integrating the US armed forces—segregation in terms of burial is immediately ended in all national cemeteries including Arlington.

1950   Over 70,000 American soldiers and servicemen have been interred at Arlington.

1955   Arlington House is designated a memorial to General Robert E. Lee.

1958   The double interment ceremonies for the World War II and Korean War Unknowns are held at the Memorial Amphitheater.

1959   The 100,000th burial takes place at Arlington in April.

1962   The policy of accepting grave reservations ends at Arlington and all national cemeteries.

1963   President John Fitzgerald Kennedy is buried at Arlington after his assassination in Dallas, Texas.

1966   During peak months, daily visitation at the cemetery reaches 50,000; Fort Myer South Post is annexed by Arlington bringing the cemetery to its current 612 acres.

1967   Two of the three *Apollo I* astronauts are interred after a launch pad fire; the John F. Kennedy memorial grave is dedicated; victims of the U.S.S. *Forrestal* fire are buried in Section 46.

1968   Senator Robert F. Kennedy is buried after his assassination.

1969   The Archbishop of Krakow, Karol Wojtyla, the future Pope John-Paul II, visits Arlington and views the coffin of Ignace Paderewski.

1970   Arlington is closed to vehicular traffic.

1971   Audie Murphy, the most decorated American soldier in World War II, is buried after his death in a plane crash; the Robert F. Kennedy gravesite is completed.

1976   Medal of Honor headstones are highlighted with gold lettering; the Historian's Office is created; Queen Elizabeth of England, King Juan Carlos of Spain, and Emperor Hirohito of Japan visit Arlington during the nation's bicentennial celebrations.

1977   Francis Gary Powers, the U-2 pilot shot down over the Soviet Union in 1960, is buried after his death in a helicopter crash.

1980   Three airmen from the aborted Iranian hostage rescue mission are laid to rest; the Columbarium for cremated remains is opened.

1981   General of the Army Omar Bradley, the last of the five star generals, is buried after a state funeral.

1983   Twenty-one soldiers killed in a terrorist bombing in Beirut, Lebanon, are interred in Section 59.

1984   The Vietnam Unknown Serviceman in interred at the Tomb of the Unknown Soldier.

1986   Dick Scobee and Michael Smith, two members of the crew of the Space Shuttle *Challenger* are buried; construction on a new visitors center is begun; Arlington completes its 200,000th burial.

1987   The *Challenger* memorial is dedicated in Section 46.

1988   The remains of Polar explorer Matthew Henson is reinterred to Arlington; the new visitors center is dedicated.

1989   Michael Gannon, one of the victims of the terrorist bombing of Pan Am Flight 103, is buried in Section 59; six of the sailors killed after a turret explosion on the U.S.S. *Iowa* are interred at Arlington.

1991   Seventeen casualties from the Persian Gulf War are buried at Arlington; nine memorial stones are erected for other military personnel whose remains were not recovered.

1992   Ignace Jan Paderewski is returned to his native Poland fifty-one years after his death.

1993   Former Justice and civil rights activist, Thurgood Marshall, is buried in Section 5; General Matthew Ridgeway, the American commander of the Eighth Army in Korea, is interred; Arlington completes its 230,000th burial; three American soldiers killed in Mogadishu, Somalia during *Operation Restore Hope* are laid to rest.

1994   Jacqueline Kennedy Onassis is interred; a memorial service is held to commemorate the 50th anniversary of the Normandy invasion.

1995   Ground breaking for the Women in Military Service Memorial; Chief Justice Warren Burger is buried; the Pan Am 103 Memorial is dedicated in Section 1.

1996   Sgt. Heather Johnsen becomes the first female badge holder.

1997   Vietnam Unknown is exhumed and later identified as Captain Michael Blassey.

1998   Two victims from the terrorist attack against the US Embassy in Nairobi are interred; two US Capitol police officers killed in the line of duty are buried.

1999   Congress authorizes the future transfer of 37 acres of land from the Navy Annex and an additional eight acres from Fort Myer to the cemetery.

2000   Four victims of the terrorist attack against the USS *Cole* in Yemen are interred; an estimated 1,100 World War II era veterans die each year in the United States causing an increased demand for grave space in national cemeteries.

2001   AA Flight 77 strikes the Pentagon killing 189 people; first victims from the terrorist attack are buried at Arlington; CIA Officer Mike Spann, the first American casualty in Afghanistan from Operation Enduring Freedom is buried; 12 acres from the National Park Service are ceded to Arlington increasing its size to 624 acres.

2002   Sgt. Jason Griffin is awarded the 500th Tomb Guard Identification badge; General Benjamin O. Davis, commander of the famed Tuskegee Airmen, is buried at Arlington; commingled and unidentified remains from the Pentagon attack are interred in Section 64; Arlington is closed to new burials in private monument sections.

2003   Famed World War II cartoonist, Bill Mauldin is laid to rest; Senator Daniel Patrick Moynihan is buried at Arlington; three of the astronauts killed during re-entry on board the Columbia are interred bring to 17 the total number of astronauts buried at Arlington; the first combat casualty from *Operation Iraqi Freedom* is buried at Arlington on April 11th; plans begin for replacement of the main marble portion of Tomb of the Unknown Soldier; the *Columbia* Memorial is approved. By year's end, 45 casualties from the Iraqi War are interred at Arlington.

2004   By May, 58 casualties from the war and insurgency in Iraq are buried at Arlington.

APPENDIX C
JOHN F. KENNEDY GRAVESITE: INSCRIPTIONS

Let the word go forth
From this time and place
To friend and foe alike
That the torch has been passed
To a new generation of Americans

Let every nation know
Whether it wishes us well or ill
That we shall pay any price—bear any burden
Meet any hardship—support any friend
Oppose any foe to assure the survival
And the success of liberty

Now the trumpet summons us again
Not as a call to bear arms—though embattled we are
But a call to bear the burden of a long twilight struggle
A struggle against the common enemies of man
Tyranny—Poverty—Disease—and War itself

In the long history of the world
Only a few generations have been granted
The role of defending freedom
In the hour of maximum danger
I do not shrink from this responsibility
I welcome it

The Energy—The Faith—The Devotion
Which we bring to this endeavor
Will light our country
And all who serve it
And the glow from that fire
Can truly light the world

And so my fellow Americans
Ask not what your country can do for you
Ask what you can do for your country
My fellow citizens of the world—ask not
What America will do for you—but what together
We can do for the freedom of man

With a good conscience our only sure reward
With history the final judge of our deeds
Let us go forth to lead the land we love—asking His blessing

And His help—but knowing that here on earth
God's work must truly be our own

Inaugural Address—January 20, 1961

Robert F. Kennedy Gravesite Inscriptions

It is from numberless diverse acts of courage and belief that human history is
shaped. Each time a man stands up for an ideal, or acts to improve the lot of others,
or strikes out against injustice, he sends forth a tiny ripple of hope, and crossing each
other from a million different centers of energy and daring, those ripples build a current that can sweep down the mightiest walls of oppression and resistance.

South Africa, 1966

Aeschylus wrote: "In our sleep, pain that cannot forget falls drop by drop upon
the heart and in our despair, against our will comes wisdom through the awful grace
of God."

What we need in the United States is not division, what we need in the United
States is not hatred, what we need in the United States is not violence or lawlessness,
but love and wisdom and compassion toward one another, and a feeling of justice
toward those who still suffer within our country, whether they be white or they be
black. Let us dedicate ourselves to what the Greeks wrote so many years ago: to tame
the savageness of man and make gentle the life of this world. Let us dedicate ourselves
to that and say a prayer for our country and people.

Indianapolis, 1968

Appendix D

ELIGIBILITY

Eligibility for In-ground Burial

The persons specified below are eligible for in-ground burial of either casketed or cremated remains at Arlington National Cemetery. The last period of active duty of former members of the Armed Forces must have ended honorably.

a. Any active duty member of the Armed Forces, except those serving on active duty for training purposes only.

b. Any veteran retired from active military service with the Armed Forces.

c. Any veteran who is retired from the Reserves is eligible upon reaching the age of 60 and who is drawing retired pay, and who served a period of active duty (other than for training).

d. Any former member of the Armed Forces separated honorably prior to October 1, 1949, for medical reasons with a 30 percent or grater disability rating effective on the day of discharge.

e. Any former member of the Armed Forces awarded one of the following decorations:
   - Medal of Honor;
   - Distinguished Service Cross (Air Force Cross or Navy Cross);
   - Distinguished Service Medal;
   - Silver Star, or,
   - Purple Heart.

f. The current and any former President of the United States.

g. Any former member of the Armed Forces who served on active duty (other than for training purposes) and held any of the following positions:
   - An elective office of the U.S. Government;
   - Office of the Chief Justice of the United States or an Associate Justice of the Supreme Court of the United States;
   - An office listed, at the time the individual held the position, in 5 USC 5312 or 5313 (Levels I and II of the Executive Schedule); or
   - The chief of a mission who at the time during his/her tenure was classified in Class I under the provision of Section 411, Act of 13 August 1946, 60 Stat. 1002, as amended (22 USC 866) or as listed in State Department memorandum dated March 21, 1988.

h. Any former prisoner of war (POW) who, while a POW, served honorably in the active military, naval or air service, whose last period of service terminated honorably and who died on or after November 30, 1993.

i. The spouse, widow or widower, minor children, permanently dependent children, and certain unmarried adult children of any of the above eligible veterans.

j. The widow or widower of:
   - A member of the Armed Forces lost or buried at sea, or officially determined missing in action;
   - A member of the Armed Forces buried in a U.S. military cemetery overseas maintained by the American Battle Monuments Commission; or

- A member of the Armed Forces interred in Arlington National Cemetery as part of a group burial.
k. The parents of a minor child, or permanently dependent child whose remains, based on the eligibility of a parent, are buried in Arlington National Cemetery. A spouse divorced form the primary eligible, or widowed and remarried, is not eligible for interment.
l. The surviving spouse, minor children, permanently dependent children, of any eligible veteran buried in Arlington National Cemetery.
m. Provided certain conditions are met, a former member of the Armed Forces may be buried in the same grave with a close relative who is buried in Arlington National Cemetery and who is the primary eligible.

Eligibility for In-ground Burial of Cremated Remains

Any veteran eligible for in-ground burial, and their dependents, may have their cremated remains placed in a designated unmarked area of the cemetery. All subsequent burials of eligible family members will also be in this area of the cemetery. The ashes must be in a biodegradable container or be placed in the gravesite without a container. A permanent register of all burials in this special area is maintained at the cemetery's Administration Building.

Eligibility for Columbarium Inurnment

The following persons are eligible for inurnment. The last period of active duty (other than for training) of former members of the Armed Forces must have ended honorably.
a. Any member of the Armed Forces who dies on active duty.
b. Any former member of the Armed Forces retired from active duty.
c. Any former member of the Armed Forces who served on active duty other than for training purposes.
d. Any member of a Reserve component of the Armed Forces who dies while:
- On active duty for training or performing full-time service under title 32, United States Code;
- Performing authorized travel to or from that duty or service;
- On authorized inactive duty training including training performed as a member of the Army National Guard or the Air National Guard (23 USC 502); or,
- Hospitalized or being treated at the expense of the United States for an injury or disease incurred or contracted while on that duty or service, performing that travel or inactive duty training, or undergoing that hospitalization or treatment at the expense of the United States.
e. Any member of the Reserve Officers' Training Corps of the Army, Navy or Air Force whose death occurs while:
- Attending an authorized training camp;
- On an authorized practice cruise;
- Performing authorized travel to or from that camp or cruise; or,
- Hospitalized or receiving treatment at the expense of the United States for injury or disease incurred while attending that camp or cruise, performing that travel, or receiving that hospitalization or treatment at the expense of the

United States.

f. Any citizen of the United States who, during any war in which the United States has been engaged, served in the Armed Forces of any government allied with the United States during that war, whose last service ended honorably by death or otherwise, and was a citizen of the United States at the time of entry into that service and at the time of death.

g. Certain commissioned officers of the National Oceanic and Atmospheric Administration, formerly the United States Coast and Geodetic Survey.

h. Certain commissioned officers of the U.S. Public Health Service.

i. Spouses, minor children and certain adult children of those listed above.

j. A former member of a group certified as active military service for the purpose of receiving benefits by the U.S. Department of Veterans Affairs by the provisions of Section 401, Public Law 95-202.

Requesting an Exception to Burial Eligibility Policies

Requests for exceptions to burial eligibility policies will not be considered until the death of the individual. A letter requesting an exception should be mailed, or faxed, to (or, for further information, contact):

Superintendent
Arlington National Cemetery
Arlington, Virginia 22211-5003
FAX (703) 697-4967

Headstone Symbols

In the newer areas of the Cemetery, only government headstones are permitted in order to maintain the uniform appearance of the sections. If an individual wishes a private marker, the grave must be located in an area that has such monuments. Private markers are provided at family expense but government headstones are supplied free of charge from the Veterans Administration. Only government niche covers are permitted in the Columbarium. Family members may choose a religious or philosophical emblem from an approved list of 26 such symbols.

1. Christian/Latin Cross
2. Wheel of Righteousness
3. Star of David (Jewish)
4. Presbyterian
5. Russian Orthodox
6. Lutheran
7. Episcopal
8. Unitarian
9. United Methodist
10. Aaronic Order
11. Mormon – Angel Moroni
12. Native American
13. Serbian Orthodox
14. Bahai
15. Atheist
16. Muslim
17. Hindu
18. Greek
19. Konko-Kyo Faith
20. Reorganized Church of Latter Day Saints
21. Sufishm Reoriented
22. Tenrikyo
23. Seicho-No-Ie
24. World Messianity (Izunome)
25. United Church of Religious Science
26. Christian Reformed Church

1

2

3

4

5

6

7

8

9

10

11

12

13

14

15

18

17

18

19

20

21

22

23

24

25

26

Appendix E
21 FACTS ABOUT ARLINGTON CEMETERY

1. Flags located in the cemetery are lowered to half-staff thirty minutes before the first burial and remain lowered until after the last funeral is completed. Flags are flown at full-staff at all other times except during periods of official mourning and on certain national holidays.

2. President John F. Kennedy made three official visits to Arlington while in office, the last on Veterans' Day, 1963, just eleven days before his assassination.

3. Mrs. Jacqueline Kennedy and Attorney General Robert F. Kennedy placed several items in the President's casket prior to burial. These include three letters, a pair of cuff links, a piece of scrimshaw engraved with the presidential seal, a silver rosary, and a PT-109 tie clasp.

4. Arlington is the only national cemetery authorized to use horses and caissons as a regular part of its funeral ceremonies. The caisson used during the funerals of Presidents Franklin D. Roosevelt and John F. Kennedy is still in daily operation.

5. The original funeral architecture from the first Kennedy gravesite is now held in storage in Boston, Massachusetts.

6. Every American president since Woodrow Wilson has visited Arlington National Cemetery at least once while in office.

7. The first national cemetery was created in 1862 at the behest of President Abraham Lincoln "…for the soldiers who shall die in the service of their country." Fourteen cemeteries were created in that year for the dead from the Civil War. Arlington was established in 1864. By 1871, the remains of 300,000 Union soldiers were buried in national cemeteries with approximately 42% individually unidentified.

8. There are currently 136 national cemeteries in the United States and Puerto Rico, providing graves for over two million American veterans. Arlington and the Soldiers Home are operated by the Department of the Army while 14 are administered by the Department of Interior and 120 under the Veterans Administration. Seventy-three of the cemeteries were created during and immediately after the American Civil War. Arlington is the best known of the national cemeteries. The largest in terms of acreage is the Calverton National Cemetery in New York consisting of over 1045 acres while the smallest in the Hampton National Cemetery with just .03 acres. The Long Island National Cemetery has the most burials with well over 322,000 interments. The Fort Sill National Cemetery in Oklahoma is the newest of the national cemeteries and was dedicated in 2001 with six additional cemeteries scheduled to open shortly to accommodate the increased need for grave space due to the aging World War II veteran population. In 2001, there were 84,000 interments in the 61 active national cemeteries.

9. Over 2,000 ceremonies are conducted at the Tomb of the Unknown Soldier annually. Foreign heads of state and dignitaries regularly place a wreath at the Tomb to honor all American veterans. During state visits, honor guard contingents from all of the Armed Services participate during the ceremonies at the Tomb.

10. Arlington currently averages 25 funerals per day, approximately 6,200 annually. The cemetery has less than 50,000 vacant graves although current efforts to acquire additional acreage from adjacent military facilities should yield an additional 30,000 plots and ensure the cemetery's ongoing operation through 2060 (each acre, depending upon its topography, can accommodate approximately 800 new graves). After the cemetery reaches its capacity, it will be closed to interments but will continue to operate as a national shrine.

11. There are 4,735 unknowns buried at Arlington, the vast majority from the Civil War. During that conflict, a soldier killed in action had a one in three chance of not being identified.

12. During the Memorial Day weekend, individual American flags are placed on all the graves by members of the 3d Infantry. The flags remain in place until after the conclusion of the Memorial Day ceremonies.

13. There are two American presidents buried at Arlington – John F. Kennedy and William Howard Taft. Taft holds the distinction of being the only person to have been both President and Chief Justice of the Supreme Court.

14. Three of the six Iwo Jima flag-raisers are interred at Arlington – Ira Hayes, Michael Strank, and Rene Gagnon.

15. Dead from every American War from the Revolution through the Persian Gulf conflict are buried at Arlington. Pre-1864 dead were reinterred after the cemetery began operations.

16. Five of the nine World War II five-star generals and admirals are buried at Arlington – Halsey, Marshall, Leahy, Arnold, and Bradley.

17. There are two mausoleums – the Miles and Sullivan – located in the cemetery. Above ground interments are no longer permitted.

18. Arlington House was converted into a monument to Robert E. Lee by act of Congress in 1955 and is administered by the National Park Service.

19. Arlington is the only national cemetery operated by the United States Army. All other cemeteries fall under the jurisdiction of the Veterans' Administration.

20. Forty-six foreign nationals from ten countries are buried at Arlington. Most were associated with embassies during wartime and died in the United States which entitled them to burial in a national cemetery. One German and two Italian prisoners-of-war were interred in accordance with the Geneva Convention which entitled captured soldiers to burial with military honors. The current breakdown is a follows: 24 British, 4 Canadian, 4 Italian, 2 Dutch, 2 South Vietnamese (unknowns), 1 South African, 1 Australian, 1 Chinese, 1 Greek, 1 German, 1 Underdetermined nationality.

21. Over 3,800 former slaves are buried at Arlington. Most fled to Washington during the Civil War to escape bondage, while others lived in the Freedmen's Village that housed some 1,100 blacks after the war. The village was located near the site of the present Memorial Amphitheater.

SELECTED BIBLIOGRAPHY

Much of the material used in the preparation of this book comes from the files at the Historian's Office at Arlington National Cemetery and the record groups of the National Archives.

Above and Beyond: A History of the Medal of Honor from the Civil War to Vietnam. Boston: Boston Publishing Company, 1985.

Arlington National Cemetery: The Official Website of Arlington National Cemetery. 22 January 2003. www.arlingtoncemetery.org.

Arlington National Cemetery. Michael Patterson. 22 January 2003. www.arlington-cemetery.com.

"*Did you know?...Army Engineers Designed and built President John F. Kennedy's Original Eternal Flame at Arlington Cemetery?* 28 May 2003. www.hq.usace.army.mil/history/vignettes/Vignette_60.htm.

Avil, Howard. *United States National Military Cemetery: Arlington Virginia.* Washington, D.C.: Levin C. Handy, 1903.

Burial and Memorial Benefits. 23 January 2003. *National Cemetery Administration.* www.cem.va.gov/facts.htm

Cabbage, Michael and William Harwood. Comm Check...The Final Flight of Shuttle Columbia. New York: Free Press, 2004.

Connelly, Thomas L. *The Marble Man: Robert E. Lee and His Image in American Society.* Baton Rouge: Louisiana State University Press, 1977.

Costanzo, Raymond. Personal Interview. 25 August 1986.

Counter, S. Allen. *North Pole Legacy: Black, White, and Eskimo.* Amherst: University of Massachusetts Press, 1991.

Dolan, Edward F. *Matthew Henson: Black Explorer. New York: Dodd, Meade & Company, 1979.

Fleming, Dan B. *...Ask What You Can Do for Your Country: The Memory and Legacy of John F. Kennedy. Clearwater, Fl.: Vandamere Press, 2002.

Flood, Charles Bracelen. *Lee: The Last Years. Boston: Houghton Mifflin Co., 1981.

Forbes-Lindsay, C. H. *Washington: The City and Seat of Government. Philadelphia:* John C. Winston, Co., 1908.

Ford, Charles R. Memorandum for the Director of the Army Staff, March 30, 1977.

Four Days. comp. By United Press International and American Heritage Magazine. New York: Simon and Schuster, 1964.

Freeman, Douglas Southall. *Robert E. Lee: A Biography. New York: Charles Scribner's Sons, 1940.*

Fuqua, Paul. Telephone Interview. 15 August 1986.

Gowen, Annie. "Father's Salute to a Son with 'a Big Heart," Washington Post. April 11, 2003, A-29, A-40.

Harrell, Lionel. Telephone Interview. 24 January 2003.

Hinkel, John Vincent. *Arlington: Monuments to Heroes. Englewood Cliffs:* Prentice-Hall, Inc., 1970.

Johnson, Lyndon. *The Vantage Point: Perspectives on the Presidency, 1963-1969.* New York: Holt, Rinehart and Winston, 1971.

Kavenaugh, James. "A Visit to the Grave." *Catholic Digest*, July 1965, pp. 8-11.

Lee, Mary Custis. 9 February 1861. Personal Letter from Arlington House. Du Pont Library. Stratford Plantation, Virginia.

Lee, Robert E. 22 November 1861. Letter to Annie and Agnes Lee. Du Pont Library, Stratford Plantation, Virginia.

Lee, Robert E. 5 April 1866. Letter to Francis S. Smith, esq. Du Pont Library. Stratford Plantation, Virginia.

MacDonald, Rose. *Mrs. Robert E. Lee.* Boston: Ginn and Company, 1939.

Mack, William P. and Royal W. Connell. *Naval Ceremonies, Customs, and Traditions.* Annapolis: Naval Institute Press, 1986.

Manchester, William. *The Death of a President.* New York: Harper & Row, 1967.

Mose, James A. *Origin and Significance of Military Customs: Including Military Miscellany of Interest to Soldiers and Civilains.* Menasha: George Banta
        Publishing Company, 1917.

Moseman, B. C. and M. W. Stark. *The Last Salute: Civil and Military Funerals,*
        1921-1969. Washington, D.C.: GPO, 1971.

"The National Geographic Society's Memorial to Peary," *National Geographic Magazine*, June 1922, pp. 639-646.

Nelligan, Murray H. "'Old Arlington': The Story of the Lee Mansion National
        Memorial." Unpublished manuscript. National Park Service, 1953.

News Archive. September 2001. Defense Link: United States Department of Defense. 22 January 2003. http://www.defenselink.mil/news/Sep2001/.

Peary, Robert E. *The North Pole: Its Discovery in 1909 Under the Auspices of the Peary Arctic Club.* New York: Frederick A. Stokes, 1910.

Powers, Dave. Personal Interview. 6 August 1986.

Robertson, James. Personal Interview. 24 June 1986.

Rose, C. B. *Arlington County Virginia: A History.* Baltimore: Port City Press, 1976.

Ross, Bill. *Iwo Jima: Legacy of Valor.* New York: Vantage Press, 1986.

Schildt, Roberta. "Freedman's Village: Arlington, Virginia, 1863-1900," *The
        Arlington Historical Magazine, 7 October 1984, pp. 11-21.*

September 11: Chronology of Terror. Cable Network News. 22 January 2003.
http://www.cnn.com/2001/US/09/11/chronology.attack/.

Templeman, Eleanor Lee. *Arlington House: Vignettes of a Virginia County.*
        Arlington: Eleanor Lee Templeman, 1959.

21 Days to Baghdad: The Inside Story of How America Won the War Against Baghdad. New York: Time Books, 2003.

Vogal, Steve. "Facing the Scene of Disaster." *Washington Post*, September 1, 2002, C-1, C-5.

_____. "Lost and, Sometimes, Never Found: Pentagon Families Bury 25 of Their Dead Together and Mourn Five Not Identified." *Washington Post*, September 13, 2002, C-1.

War Against Terror. Cable News Network. 12 January 2003.
<http://www.cnn.com/SPECIALS/2001/trade.center/victims/AA77-victims.html>.

White, Josh. "'Our Heroic Columbia Astronauts' Seven on Shuttle Remembered at Arlington Cemetery Ceremony. *Washington Post*, February 3, 2004, B-1, B-8.

Wilson, Eugene H. Personal Interview. 31 July 1986.

The WPA Guide to Washington, DC. By the Federal Writers' Project. New York: Pantheon Books, 1983.

Miscellaneous

An outstanding website on the history of Arlington National Cemetery is maintained by Michael Patterson and can be accessed at:
http://www.arlingtoncemetery.net

To schedule an interment at Arlington, call 703-607-8585. The official cemetery website which included current eligibility requirements is located at:
http://www.arlingtoncemetery.org

Chris Cross Photography provides outstanding professional video and photography for interments and ceremonies at Arlington National Cemetery.
Chris Cross Commercial Photography Inc
5416 Littleford Street
North Springfield, VA 22151
USA
Telephone: 1-703-256-8842

INDEX